UNION MADE

LABOR LEADER SAMUEL GOMPERS AND HIS FIGHT FOR WORKERS' RIGHTS

Norman H. Finkelstein

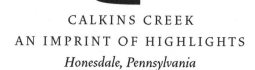

CALKINS CREEK
AN IMPRINT OF HIGHLIGHTS
Honesdale, Pennsylvania

In Loving Memory of

Sydney Finkelstein
(1908–1997)
Secretary-Treasurer and Business Agent
Wool Sorters' Union
AFL Local 22114

For information about permission to reproduce selections from this book,
please contact permissions@highlights.com.

Calkins Creek
An Imprint of Highlights
815 Church Street
Honesdale, Pennsylvania 18431
calkinscreekbooks.com
Printed in China

ISBN: 978-1-62979-638-3 (hardcover)
ISBN: 978-1-68437-626-1 (eBook)

Library of Congress Control Number: 2018955600

First edition
10 9 8 7 6 5 4 3 2 1

The type is set in Bodoni Egyptian Pro.

CONTENTS

ONE: "A Prince in My Own Realm" 5

TWO: "No More Talk—We Mean Business" 17

THREE: "Full of Fire and Dreams" 27

FOUR: "What Does Labor Want?" 37

FIVE: Struggles and Challenges 49

SIX: Gaining Respect 57

SEVEN: Labor Goes to War 71

EIGHT: Fighter for Freedom 83

Epilogue 94

Author's Note 97

Timeline 98

Source Notes 100

Bibliography 106

Index 108

Picture Credits 112

ONE

"A PRINCE IN MY OWN REALM"

"I loved the Freedom of that work."

—Samuel Gompers

Although London's East End and New York City's Lower East Side are separated by 3,500 miles of Atlantic Ocean, they are much the same. While some of their streets today contain popular restaurants and shops, both areas continue to house immigrant families much as they did two centuries ago. What has changed are the languages spoken and the backgrounds of the newcomers. What hasn't changed is the hope those people had for better lives.

Samuel Gompers was born in Spitalfields, a section of London's East End, on January 27, 1850. One of his earliest memories was of "endless rows of shabby houses bordered by pavements—nothing else, no trees, no green grass, no flowers." He was the first child of Solomon and Sarah Gompers, who had come to England from Holland. Over the next few years, the family grew with the addition of five more children: Henry, Alexander, Louis, Harriett, and Jacob. Their home at 2 Fort Street was

a two-room apartment on the first floor of a three-story, very worn brick house. Sam's grandparents lived on the floor above them. The larger room in his family's apartment served as the "sitting-room, bedroom, dining-room, and kitchen." The smaller one was used mainly for storage during the winter and as a makeshift bedroom for the children during the summer. Bath time for the children meant dragging a washtub into the center of the larger room. Water was brought in from a barrel in the backyard.

Behind the Gompers family's house stood a silk factory. Spitalfields was home to a large population of Huguenots—Protestant refugees who fled France for religious freedom. Many of them were talented silk weavers, a trade passed down from generation to generation. As handweavers were being replaced by newly invented machines, Sam witnessed the suffering and resulting poverty of his neighbors. The image of despairing workers unable to provide for their families remained with him for the rest of his life.

Many Dutch immigrants in Spitalfields, including Sam's father, were cigar makers. The tobacco was imported from America and stored in large, secure warehouses by the docks. Some of the cigar makers worked in area factories. Others, like Sam's father, worked at home. Manufacturers bought the tobacco and distributed it to the workers, who were paid by the number of cigars they produced. The cigar makers worked long hours for small wages. Naturally, the faster they worked, the more cigars they produced. But the manufacturers were not concerned only about speed. They would not pay for a poorly constructed cigar. With practice, a worker could roll perfect cigars almost automatically without much thought.

At the age of six, Sam became a student at the Jews' Free School in Bell Lane. The school provided him with a well-rounded education in mathematics, reading, writing, and geography. He was a good student and enjoyed learning, but his formal education ended just four years later when his father, despite the pleading of Sam's teacher, pulled the boy out of school to go to work. There was no other way to support the financially struggling family.

Sam, now age ten, was apprenticed to a shoemaker. The shop was noisy, and Sam was unhappy, so his father offered him another choice. Following in his father's footsteps, he became a cigar maker's apprentice. Always seeking to expand his knowledge, Sam began attending the Night Free School at this time. There he took classes in several subjects, including French.

Although the Gompers family was Jewish, they were not strictly observant. Yet young Sam came away from his spotty formal education with a good knowledge of the Hebrew language and the Talmud, the body of Jewish law and tradition. To him, however, instead of strict religious observance, service to others was "the great spiritual purpose that illumines life."

Young Sam enjoyed his leisure time. He attended theater and concerts, which led to a lifelong love of music. Sometimes he and his friends would save their pennies to buy tickets. Other times Sam's grandfather would treat him to a show.

Even as young Sam improved his cigar-making skills, he did not earn enough money to solve his family's financial problems. Other cigar makers suffered, too,

Daily prayer service at the Jews' Free School

since the Civil War then raging in America lowered the amount of imported tobacco. As unemployment grew in British cigar factories, many workers saw America as a land of hope despite the war. A popular song in the cigar shops was "To the West, To the West, To the Land of the Free." The Cigar Makers' Society had the same vision. As a labor union, it was responsible for paying unemployment benefits to a fast-growing number of unemployed members. To save money in the long run, the society offered to make small, onetime payments to members who wished to immigrate to America. For the Gompers family, this was just the motivation—and just enough cash—to leave Europe for a better life in the New World.

The family arrived at Castle Garden, on the southernmost tip of Manhattan, on July 30, 1863, aboard an old sailing vessel, the *London*. For seven weeks, they had lived below decks, crowded together with the other steerage passengers. Each family was responsible for preparing their own meals. With Sam's mother seasick throughout the journey, cooking duties were left to his father. An African crew member who befriended the family came to their rescue and helped them prepare meals. Thirteen-year-old Sam later recalled the one cheerful moment of the voyage, when the ship's captain allowed the steerage passengers on deck to join in a Fourth of July celebration, complete with music and fireworks.

The family's first experience on American soil was less than welcoming. Between July 13 and 16, New York City had been rocked by extremely violent riots protesting the planned drafting of soldiers into the Union army. The rioting turned ugly as mobs turned their anger against African Americans. Buildings were burned, and protesters' fears that blacks threatened white jobs led to a race riot. Innocent black people were attacked, and

ARRIVAL AT CASTLE GARDEN

Until the opening of Ellis Island in 1892, Castle Garden was the official immigrant gateway to New York City. It was here that the Gompers family entered the United States.

some were even hanged. Two weeks later, the tensions between blacks and whites still lingered. As Sam's father shook hands with the African crewman after disembarking and thanked him for aiding his family, a menacing mob threatened to hang them both. Solomon Gompers calmed the crowd by explaining that he was only thanking the man for being so helpful. "Any one of you," he told them, "would have done the same."

The Gompers family's new home was a four-room apartment on the Lower East Side—much more space for the family of eight than their apartment in London. The front of the building faced a slaughterhouse; the rear, a brewery. Amid the sounds and the smells, the family settled into their new life in America.

Young Sam enjoyed the adventure of exploring the streets and theaters of New York and making new friends. He was not a large person, but he had a magnetic personality that drew people to him. He expanded his education by attending lectures and classes at the Cooper Union, which provided free classes for working people. Always enjoying a good argument, he helped organize a debating club, the Arion Base Ball and Social Club, where the discussions and debates helped

This illustration is a tribute to Peter Cooper, founder of the Cooper Union. Cooper's statue is surrounded by working-class men and women and disadvantaged youths flocking to the Cooper Union to get an education.

Sam develop public-speaking skills and overcome his stuttering.

Sam's cigar-making career, begun in his London home, continued in the family apartment in New York. He and his father sat side by side rolling cigars at a table. While they worked, they talked and sang, and young Sam soon became an accomplished cigar maker. In 1864, at the age of fourteen, he became a member of Cigar Makers' Local Union No. 15. He was not interested in union affairs, but joined only to honor his father's wishes and support fellow cigar makers.

Although craft unions had existed even before the Civil War, they were largely local. In 1864, several local cigar makers' unions from around the country established the Cigar Makers' National Union. Early unions were not very powerful or well organized. Without collective bargaining between workers and bosses, employers set wages and working conditions on their own. The main way for workers to challenge their bosses was by withholding their labor and going out on strike.

Even though Sam followed news of the Civil War, which was drawing to a close in 1865, it had little direct impact on his life. But the assassination of President Abraham Lincoln in April of that year did. Even as a young boy in London, Sam had heard about Lincoln and the evils of slavery. For days after the president's death, Sam "felt that some great power for good had gone out of the world." When Lincoln's body arrived in New York on the way to its burial in Illinois, Sam stood in line for hours "for the privilege of looking upon his face." That memory stayed with him for the rest of his life.

Sam enjoyed working with his father at home, but at the age of sixteen he decided to move on. New government rules began to complicate cigar making by specifying the quantity of tobacco in a cigar and the types of boxes in which cigars had to be packed. They also added the requirement that official tax stamps had to be placed on every cigar box. It made sense for workers, like Sam, to move from home production to organized factories, often called shops.

Tenement workers were engaged in other occupations besides making cigars. Here, an entire family is shown cracking pecans in a New York tenement house in 1913.

Cigar smoking was popular well into the twentieth century. Its popularity declined as smoking was connected with a variety of health problems. Stores like this one in New York City were common in the streets of American cities.

Conditions in cigar shops varied. In most, tobacco dust swirled through the air over workers seated at uncomfortable workbenches and tables. Bathrooms were primitive and unsanitary. Lighting was haphazard. In Michael Stachelberg's factory, where Sam got his first job, dozens of workers were crammed into a large, dirty room. Sam was young and brash, willing to speak out forcefully to protest unfair actions such as lowering wages or lengthening the workday. The workers quickly recognized Sam's fearless self-confidence and chose him to present their complaints to the boss. One day, Stachelberg pointed Sam out to a visitor and said, "That is Mr. Gompers. . . . He is an agitator, but I don't give a damn, for he makes me good cigars."

The cigar-making process was similar in all the shops. Lower-paid workers called strippers prepared the tobacco. They pulled leaves from stems and bundled the leaves into piles for the cigar makers. A skilled maker could nimbly create a cigar in seconds. "A leaf of tobacco was spread out on the bench and [the worker] then made gashes in the leaf. The next step was to take a few fragments of the tobacco leaf and roll them up to form a cigar, place it against a guide and cut it to a given length and lastly take a narrow strip of tobacco leaf and roll the cigar up into it in a spiral then twist it at one end." Sam later recalled, "I loved the touch of soft velvety tobacco and gloried in the deft sureness with which I could make cigars grow in my fingers."

The repetitive nature of the cigar makers' work could be mind-numbing. So, while they worked, they talked, debated, and sang. The room they worked in may have been dingy and crowded, but their conversations were interesting and uplifting. In some shops, a worker with a good voice was chosen to read out loud from newspapers or books to the others working at their benches. Everyone in the shop supported the reader with a percentage of their cigars. Sam often filled the position

Women and children worked long hours stripping tobacco leaves from their stems, preparing the leaves for cigar makers.

of reader, perfecting the speaking skills he would use throughout his life. No topic was off-limits, and what he read increased his knowledge and his curiosity. Young Sam received an informal education at work that covered the worlds of politics, literature, and current events.

A popular topic of the day was the effect of technology on employment. New inventions and techniques were revolutionizing entire industries. Mass production lowered prices, making items that were once luxuries available to average consumers. American families could now afford clothes, shoes, and household goods that had previously been too expensive for them to buy. The downside was that fewer experienced workers were required to produce those items because the new machines did not require skilled people to operate them. With millions of immigrants arriving in the United States, there was no lack of unskilled workers whom factory owners could hire at lower salaries to replace higher-paid, skilled workers.

While Sam had many friends in Mr. Stachelberg's shop, one in particular attracted his attention. Like him, Sophia Julian had been born in London to Jewish parents who had come to England from Holland. Also like him, she was sixteen years old. Her job was to strip tobacco leaves from their stems. Sam and Sophia spent time together outside of work as well. They walked, went to the theater, and picnicked. Although Sophia lived with her parents in Brooklyn, she often came into Manhattan to attend his debate club meetings. Two or three times a week after work, Sam traveled to Brooklyn to visit Sophia. Getting to and from Brooklyn was not easy and involved both a ferry and a stagecoach. If Sam stayed too long in Brooklyn and missed a connection, his trip home would include a five-mile walk in the dark from the ferry.

On January 26, 1867, at Sam's seventeenth birthday celebration, one of his friends playfully suggested that Sam and Sophia should get married. The next morning, without telling their parents, they went to Brooklyn City Hall and were married by a justice of the peace. To celebrate their marriage, they shared an inexpensive lunch and went to a play at the Park Theatre, just across from City Hall, where they saw a drama called *Poudrette; or, Under the Snow*. That evening, they returned separately to their parents' homes.

It wasn't long before the young couple moved into the Gompers household, but they quickly saved enough money to rent their own two-room apartment a block and a half away. Sam, proud of his new independence, boasted that he paid cash for their furniture. Within a year, however, he lost his job at Stachelberg's shop, and rather than fight the competition for jobs in the city, he decided to leave Manhattan. The couple moved to Hackensack, New

Jersey, where cigar factory jobs were more available. When their first child was about to be born, Sophia returned to Sam's parents' home, where their son, also named Samuel, was born on September 4, 1868.

To protect his growing family, Sam joined the Hand-in-Hand Society, one of the many *Landsmanschaftn*, or mutual aid societies, formed by Jewish immigrants in America. These societies provided members with medical care, small interest-free loans, and free burials.

In 1872, Sam became an American citizen. Proudly, he cast his first vote for president that year, for Ulysses S. Grant. Years later, when a congressman questioned him about his nationality, Sam proudly responded, "I am an American in every thing that goes to make up an American except birth."

Sam's interests expanded to include active membership in two fraternal organizations, the Ancient Order of Foresters and the Independent Order of Odd Fellows. Through their rituals and lectures, Sam developed a strong belief in his duty to care for others. He was an active participant in lodge activities and was elected to high office as his friendships, social connections and self-confidence grew. People liked him and he liked them, and leadership positions came easily to him. "I never was an aspirant for any office in my life," he later wrote. "Office came to me always, I never went after it."

Although cigar makers like Sam preferred working close to home, wage reductions, labor disputes, and strikes often made it necessary for them to move around. During the early years of his marriage, Sam was frequently away from home in Manhattan for weeks or months at a time as he looked for work opportunities elsewhere. At that time, there were over 10,000 cigar factories in the United States. Sam had a good reputation as an accomplished cigar maker, and it was not hard for him to find a job. One benefit of his time away was the growing number of friends he made in the shops where he worked.

Sam continually worried about family finances because his wages did not always cover their household expenses. Sometimes Sophia was forced to turn to the Hand-in-Hand Society for short-term loans to pay for food and rent. Ultimately, not happy being separated from his family, he returned home in 1873.

Although Sam remained a member of the Cigar Makers' International Union, he rarely attended meetings or thought about union affairs. All that changed in 1873, when he began working in a shop in New York City owned by David Hirsch. Hirsch, an immigrant from Germany, was a socialist, as were many of his employees. Unlike the American capitalist system, in which private owners ran businesses for profit, socialism favored government or worker ownership. From his first day in Hirsch's

Whether in large or small shops, cigar workers prided themselves on their cigar-making skills.

shop, Sam listened intently to the lively conversations of his fellow workers. This was a time of conflicting thoughts about how best to win workers' rights, and for Sam it was a time to figure out his own path. This he did with the help of Karl Laurrell, an experienced labor activist, who became Sam's friend and teacher. From him, Sam learned about collective bargaining and that representatives of labor groups could sit down with their bosses to peacefully negotiate agreements about wages and better working conditions.

Laurrell introduced Sam to the teachings of European socialists such as Karl Marx and Friedrich Engels, who advocated public ownership of businesses and a classless society. Laurrell encouraged Sam to attend political meetings to better understand different political theories but advised him not to join any of the groups. At these meetings, Sam heard from radical socialists and communists, who took the teachings of Marx and Engels one step further by calling for violence and revolution. Sam was not convinced that violence could improve workers' lives. He considered all the theories and then followed Laurrell's simple advice: "Study your union card, Sam, and if the idea doesn't square with that, it ain't true."

Based on that advice, Sam understood that unions should be free from political connections and teachings and that they should exist only to improve workers' lives directly. Unions had to focus on "the relations between those associated together in making things, and proper compensation for such service." He began to realize that the only way to improve working conditions was peacefully within the capitalist system through collective bargaining with employers, with the strike used only as a weapon of last resort. Confident in his own work experience and the education he received in the shops, Sam turned his full attention to the union. For him, "life was becoming more real and more serious."

Young children often worked alongside adults in cigar factories. Here, they are shown in the sausage department of Armour & Company's meatpacking house in Chicago in 1893.

TWO
"NO MORE TALK—WE MEAN BUSINESS"

"Eight hours for work. Eight hours for rest. Eight hours for what we will."

—Banner slogan

There were not enough hours in the day for Sam as he balanced work, family responsibilities, and union involvement. "He found what he called the great fact of his life—the trade union. It fascinated him and consumed his time." More and more, he found himself drawn to his fellow union members, and his mind was filled with ideas about how to improve their lives. He also understood that to move forward successfully, he needed to understand the history of American labor.

In early America, farmers, blacksmiths, shoemakers, grocers, and bakers were self-employed. As the country grew, so did the demand for goods. By the time of the American Revolution, small shops and factories employed skilled workers to produce everything from clothes to tools. As immigration to the United States increased, so did the number and size of manufacturing plants to supply goods to the exploding population.

From time to time, skilled workers in a single trade banded together to improve working conditions. They tried to get owners to agree to shorter working hours and to increase wages, but they often lacked the power to succeed. Workers had one important way to make their points, however: to stop working, or strike. Although workers did not get paid during a strike, shop owners also lost money. A strike ended when one side—usually the workers—hurt the most. One of the first successful strikes in American history occurred in Philadelphia in 1786 when the city's printers walked out of their shops to protest a lowering of their weekly wages. The strike worked, and the employers restored the workers' pay.

Going out on strike sometimes landed workers in court. Refusing to work and convincing other workers to join a strike was once considered a crime. In 1806, striking shoemakers were convicted of criminal conspiracy in Philadelphia. When workers at the Thompsonville Carpet Manufacturing Company in Connecticut went out on strike in 1834, they were arrested for striking. After two prolonged trials, they were found not guilty. That court case finally made it clear that it was not illegal for workers to join together to fight for their rights.

Slowly, laws changed to benefit some workers. By the 1830s, the customary workday for most workers was ten hours, except for federal government employees,

Samuel Gompers, about 1884. At age thirty-four he was already a well-known union activist.

who worked twelve hours a day. After a successful strike by government workers in 1836, President Martin Van Buren made the ten-hour day official for them in 1840. Child labor was another problem. In 1842, the Commonwealth of Massachusetts set the minimum age for factory workers at fifteen. Yet even though laws like these existed, they were not always enforced.

As local businesses evolved into national corporations, and railroads made it easier for goods made in one city to be sold throughout the country, workers formed national unions. They were responding to a new world in which skilled workers faced lower wages, longer workdays, and the arrival of untrained immigrants willing to accept lower pay. In 1866 a group of workers formed the National Labor Union to create the country's first major national union. The union had ambitious plans beyond workers' wages and the eight-hour workday, including equal rights for all, free land for farmers, and the creation of worker-owned businesses called cooperatives. Members even formed their own political party. The union ultimately received little support because of its unrealistic mission, and it disbanded six years later.

A more successful group, the Knights of Labor, was founded in 1869. Unlike the National Labor Union, the Knights of Labor worked within the existing American political system and focused more directly on workers' rights. The Knights began as a secret society of tailors in Philadelphia. By 1885, they claimed a national membership of over 700,000 workers. "We mean to uphold the dignity of labor, to affirm the nobility of all who earn their bread by the sweat of their brows," the Knights declared in material given to members. But unlike specific craft unions like the Cigar Makers'

From the beginning, unions urged consumers to buy products produced by fairly treated workers. This is one of the early AFL union labels. *Labor Omnia Vincit* means "work conquers all," which became an early motto of the AFL.

International Union, the Knights welcomed all workers, skilled and unskilled. While their goal was to provide workers with self-respect, they did not believe in using the strike as a weapon against employers.

Sam joined the Knights while working in Hirsch's shop but never became an active member. He agreed with their main goals, such as the eight-hour workday, an end to child labor, equal pay for men and women, and payment for job-related injuries. But he had trouble with their policy of opening membership to everyone involved in a trade, skilled or not. He thought that skilled workers like himself deserved their own benefits and protections and should not be lumped together with unskilled workers. He also disagreed with the Knights' no-strike policy, since to him, the strike, when used wisely, was the ultimate weapon workers had against their employers.

The 1870s were a period of economic depression in the United States. Businesses closed, workers were fired, and employers reduced the wages of those who remained. Unemployed workers demonstrated in the

Unemployed workers gathered in New York City's Tompkins Square Park in 1874 to solicit help from the city to pay for rent and food. Sam was at the demonstration and just barely escaped injury as police drove away demonstrators.

streets, sometimes violently. Sam participated in protest meetings and marches. In 1871, he walked in a parade of 25,000 workers in New York City advocating for an eight-hour workday. Even as he protested, he realized that obtaining benefits for workers during an economic downturn would not be easy. The best time to win labor victories was when the economy was thriving. But that did not mean workers should give up fighting for their rights. It was particularly during bad times that workers should band together and show unity.

In the early 1870s, there were over 14,000 registered cigar makers in the New York City area, with thousands more not registered. Only 1,500 of them belonged to local unions. Within a few years, due in part to the worsening economic conditions, union membership dropped dramatically.

On January 13, 1874, thousands of unemployed workers in many trades assembled in New York City's Tompkins Square Park to protest the lack of public aid for the large number of poor, unemployed residents. Their families were hungry and being forced from their homes because they couldn't pay their rent.

Organizers of the protest received permits from the police, but city leaders feared possible violence at a gathering of so many angry unemployed workers. The city canceled the permits just as the rally was scheduled to begin. Unaware of the city's actions, demonstrators continued to pour into the park. Without warning, mounted police charged into the crowd, swinging clubs and thrashing men, women, and children.

Sam, who arrived as the attack began, recalled, "It was an orgy of brutality. I was caught in the crowd on the street and barely saved my head from being cracked by jumping down a cellarway." Over forty demonstrators were arrested, mostly unemployed immigrants. Many others were injured. The violence frightened ordinary citizens who incorrectly blamed lawless immigrant radicals for the rioting. The next day, the *New York Times* reported, "The persons arrested yesterday seem all to have been foreigners—chiefly Germans or Irishmen. Communism is not a weed of native growth."

Around the country, strikes over increased mechanization, poor working conditions, and declining wages were taking place. Negative public reaction to the Tompkins Square Park riot and violent incidents in other cities made Sam realize that to succeed, unions could not become associated with radical political groups that challenged traditional American values.

At the same time, changes in the cigar-making industry threatened the future of Sam's union. First, newly arrived immigrants who made cigars using molds began replacing highly skilled union workers. The invention of a cigar-molding device in 1869 made it possible for an unskilled worker to form cigars easily. Cigar makers viewed this as a threat not only to their status as highly trained workers but also to their incomes. The union members' hand-rolled workmanship was a result of years of apprenticeship, training, and experience. They could not accept as equals the poorly trained and poorly paid immigrants working with molds. The members of Sam's union, the Cigar Makers' International Union Local 15, held firm and would not allow mold users to join.

Sam did not oppose progress. He understood that skilled workmanship had to coexist with mechanization and that all workers should be treated with respect. In 1872, he joined a new union, the United Cigar Makers of New York (UCMNY), which invited mold workers into its membership. The union had been organized three years earlier by Adolph Strasser, who would become Sam's friend, colleague, and adviser.

Manufacturers soon discovered another cheap way to make cigars. They bought or leased old, run-down tenement buildings on the Lower East Side, then offered apartments at low cost to immigrant families who agreed to make cigars for them at home using the mold method. In effect, the manufacturers made money in two ways—from the cigars and from the workers' rent. After paying for their raw material (the tobacco) and rent, and even after enlisting other family members to join them in working long hours, the cigar makers usually had little money left for food and other necessities.

Some manufacturers still took pride in the hand-rolled cigars they produced and criticized cigars made with molds. The owner of a cigar company where Sam once worked told the *New York Times*, "The cigars so made are of the poorest grade . . . inasmuch as [their] manufacture in cramped dwelling apartments, where the leaves must be assorted on the floor of the room in which often a family eat and sleep, must be attended with much uncleanness, and even with the spread often of infectious disease."

The terrible conditions the tenement workers faced stirred Sam to action. He applied the organizational skills he had learned from his lodge activities to union activism. His days were now filled with work and union affairs. Usually getting little sleep, he spent all day at his regular job and then spent nights writing pamphlets, speaking to groups, and convincing others to join the union. He often found himself socializing late at night over a beer and using his powers of persuasion to convince a single cigar maker to become a union member. In 1873, he traveled to Washington, DC, as part of a union delegation to meet with President Ulysses S. Grant for a discussion on the eight-hour workday. When Sam stood up to leave, Grant put his hand on the union leader's shoulder and said, "You are not a very tall man, Mr. Gompers." Sam, even then never at

Families such as this one in 1877 New York City often worked together in their homes making cigars using the mold method. How fast they worked and how perfect their cigars were determined their income.

a loss for words, replied to the five-foot-eight Grant, "Yes, but I am not the President of the United States."

In 1875, the Cigar Makers' International Union of America admitted the UCMNY into its membership as Local 144. Sam's fellow members recognized his abilities and dedication and elected him president of the new local. He was twenty-five years old. His friend Adolph Strasser was elected financial secretary.

With that recognition, Sam set out to improve working conditions for all cigar makers in New York City, both skilled and unskilled. He created rules that forced Local 144 to conduct its business fairly and democratically. He required members to first obtain permission from the union before going out on strike, thereby avoiding expensive strikes they had no hope of winning. He instituted secret ballots to determine important actions so all members felt free to offer their opinions. He urged increases in dues to provide financial assistance to workers and their families in the event of a strike, illness, or death. Membership grew, and with it the reputation of the local union and its president.

Sam's new activism gave him further

insight into the need for unions. As Local 144's president, he wrote a letter to George Hurst, the national president of the Cigar Makers' International Union of America, describing conditions in New York City:

"When we see on the one hand the factories decreasing, and hand work with it, and many out of employment, on the other the tenement houses with its thousands crowded together, like hogs in a pen [only the hogs have the advantage they need not work] working from 16 to 20 hours a day, producing treble the number of Cigars, that they properly should, it compels us to ask ourselves the question, what shall we do to alter or prevent its further growth? I will answer, join your Trade Union."

Thanks to Sam's leadership, Local 144 became the largest local in the country, with over 250 members. Union leaders recognized his accomplishments and appointed him their unpaid national organizer, responsible for growing union membership across the country. Not only did he now work his normal ten-hour day rolling cigars, but, with no additional pay, he also wrote and delivered union leaflets, spoke frequently at union meetings, and maintained contact with cigar makers across the country. Sometimes his travel involved overnight stays away from home, paid for out of his own pocket.

Although his life revolved around work, union, and home, Sam did manage to find time for other interests. He enjoyed music and even took violin lessons early in his working career. He taught himself German by reading German newspapers with a dictionary by his side. Working in shops with Cuban cigar makers, he picked up conversational Spanish. He also enjoyed playing a game of pool or billiards with friends.

By 1877, working conditions for the tenement cigar makers in New York had worsened. Employers steadily reduced the number of workers while keeping the same workload and lowering the wages of those who remained. With no alternative available to improve their lives, workers went on strike. The bosses responded by evicting them and their families from their tenement apartments.

Sam understood the importance of unity and encouraged skilled cigar makers throughout the city to join the strike and support the tenement workers. At the same time, union members hoped to improve working conditions for all cigar makers, including themselves. Sam called for a mass organizational meeting on October 14 to vote on a general strike. He organized picket lines and set down rules about behavior and demonstrating within the law. Some manufacturers, trying to break the union's spirit, closed their shops and locked out their employees. Over 11,000 strikers effectively shut down nearly all cigar manufacturing in New York City. Sam led the members of Local 144 in setting up soup kitchens, providing financial support to strikers, and even renting empty apartments for their families. But union funds were not unlimited, and the local turned to other cigar makers' unions around the country for financial support.

To provide employment for a small number of strikers, the Local 144 arranged to borrow one manufacturer's closed factory and create its own cigar-making business. At the other workers' insistence, Sam became the superintendent. The union-owned factory employed nearly seven hundred on-strike workers at its height. Everyone, including Sam, donated a percentage of their wages to help unemployed strikers and their families. The factory was two and a half miles from Sam's home. He walked to and from work because he couldn't afford the streetcar fare.

Sam believed strongly that the mission of a union was to support members in times of need. As the strike dragged on through the winter of 1877, the Local 144 was running out of money and could help fewer and fewer members. In the end, with no victory in sight, the striking workers had no alternative but to return to work. Some achieved small gains in working conditions or wages, but these were not enough to make up for the money lost during the prolonged strike.

When the strike was over, Sam soon discovered that manufacturers blacklisted strike leaders like himself, refusing to hire them. The Gompers family, which had experienced the loss of several newborns, now included five small children—Samuel, Rosetta (Rose), Henry, Abraham (Abe), and Alexander. They were impoverished. Sam, unable to find work, pawned nearly all their possessions, including his winter coat, to put food on the table. Sometimes the only meal Sophia could prepare was a thin soup containing water, flour, salt, and pepper. When Alexander was born in February 1878, Sam had no money. Since the Hand-in-Hand Society doctor was not available to aid in the birth, Sam rushed to another nearby doctor for help. The doctor refused because Sam could not pay. Enraged and fearful for his wife and newborn, Sam threatened the doctor with bodily harm until he agreed to help.

Finally, after four months of hardship, a sympathetic manufacturer, Matthew Hutchinson, offered Sam a job in his Manhattan factory. To Hutchinson, Sam's reputation as a good cigar maker meant more than his union involvement. The Gompers family was living in Manhattan at the time, but to save money, they moved across the East River to Brooklyn. The constant travel to and from work on foot and by ferry, as well as the long trip back to Brooklyn late at night after union meetings, took its toll on Sam. After just a few weeks, he moved the family back to Manhattan.

Although the 1877 strike was a failure, Sam had learned an important lesson for the future: only by uniting could workers press their demands for fair treatment.

Under Sam's leadership, Local 144 had proudly stood up for its beliefs. For a long time, it had been able to support and feed members and their families. And in the end, manufacturers—who also had lost money—gained respect for the union. The strike taught both sides that in future labor disputes, collective bargaining was the preferred way to reach an agreement. Striking must be the last resort.

The strike was a turning point for Sam. Confident in his family's unquestioning support and in his own abilities, he allowed the union to take over his life. According to one writer, "It provided him with occupation, avocation, entertainment, support for his ego, and an outlet for his powerful ambitions." His real struggle for workers' rights was about to begin.

THREE
"FULL OF FIRE AND DREAMS"

"Never permit sentiment to lead you, but let intellect dominate action."

—Karl Laurrell

Although the 1877 cigar makers' strike did not fully succeed, national union leaders took notice of Sam's hard work as president of Local 144. As a delegate to the Cigar Makers' International Union yearly conventions, he was already known for his outspoken proposals to improve workers' rights. He made his voice heard in committee meetings and on the convention floor. He was a strong speaker and a good storyteller able to hold the attention of listeners, who were impressed with his energy and leadership skills. "When I enter a fight," he said, "I expect to see it through."

It took several years for his stubbornness and strong arguments to prevail. While other union leaders sought to increase the number of members by lowering membership dues, he fought for higher dues. By 1880, the cigar makers' union adopted his suggestion. Members paid more in annual dues, but their benefits now included funds to pay them when they were unemployed, injured, or sick. In the event of death, their families received death benefits. A transportation fund provided money for workers who moved from one city to another in search of jobs. Sam assured members who disagreed with the increase in dues that "there is not a dollar which the working man and woman pays into an organization of labor which does not come back a hundredfold."

He urged the national union to adopt a revolutionary stand on equality. "No local union shall permit the rejection of an applicant for membership on account of sex, color, or system of work." That last phrase referred to tenement workers. Sam could not forget their harsh lives and working conditions. With the support of the national union, Sam ramped up his campaign against the tenement cigar factories in New York. Only now, instead of another strike, Sam turned to public action and government legislation.

Standing by his side in this fight was his friend Adolph Strasser, who became president of the Cigar Makers' International Union of America in 1877 and moved its headquarters from Chicago to New York City. The union arranged mass meetings of workers to continue protesting against tenement factories. At one such meeting on March 31, 1882, over 3,000 people crowded into the Cooper Union, bearing signs with slogans such as "Tenement-house Cigar-making Breeds Small-pox"

and "Two Companions—Tenement-house Cigars and Filth."

But signs and meetings were not enough. Strasser and Sam took frequent boat trips up the Hudson River to the state capital, Albany, where they lobbied state legislators to enact strict rules about tenement-made cigars. To strengthen their case, they needed to present solid eyewitness information. Sam took on the role of investigator to visit the tenements and report what he saw. To gain entry into people's homes, he disguised himself as a bookseller carrying Charles Dickens novels. He never sold a single book but easily acquired the access he needed to document conditions in the tenement apartments.

As a result of his visits, Sam reported that "a typical family lived in three rooms: a bedroom, a room where cigars were made, and a kitchen. Usually the entire family was engaged in the process of making cigars. Because they were paid by the cigar, life was reduced to rolling cigars for twelve hours—or more—a day, then sleeping, and waking in order to make more cigars." Sam revealed these terrible and unhealthy conditions. "Tobacco in every stage of preparation is found in all the rooms; mostly it lies spread out over the floor to dry. In the bedroom, we find casks, chests, and rusty milk cans that contain tobacco and tobacco stalks."

Sam was not alone in publicizing the dreadful conditions. Another investigator, working independently, was Clare de

Graffenried of the United States Department of the Interior's Bureau of Labor. The bureau's mission was to investigate working conditions, and de Graffenried confirmed Sam's findings by observing, "Tobacco was everywhere. Children delve into it, roll in it, sleep beside it. The dust seasons their food and befouls the water they drink, and the hands of the mother are seldom washed when she leaves the cigar table to prepare meals."

In Albany, Sam befriended a young assemblyman from New York City named Theodore Roosevelt, who, seeing a politically popular issue, took up the cause and visited the tenements with him. In the legislature, there was much opposition from cigar manufacturers who wanted the profitable tenement factories to continue. Discussion about the issue took time, and Sam returned often to Albany to testify before committees. Realizing that he could not succeed on his own, he encouraged newspaper editors, government officials, and public-spirited citizens to get involved. Social workers and health professionals also spoke out about tenement conditions, and newspaper articles kept readers informed.

After much political debate, the legislature finally passed a law in 1883 that was signed by Governor Grover Cleveland. In part it said, "The manufacture of cigars or preparation of tobacco in any form, in any room or apartments which, in the city of New York, are used as dwellings, for the purpose of living, sleeping or doing any household work therein, is hereby prohibited." While the union tried to make sure that the law was enforced, the manufacturers appealed to the courts to overturn it.

Sam's initial joy soon gave way to disappointment when the tenement law was found to be unconstitutional because it deprived workers of the right to work within their own homes—never mind the conditions under which they worked. The courts ruled that no one could interfere with the sanctity of the home and the right of individuals to choose what went on there. When Sam understood that legislation was no longer an option, he turned to a last resort of strikes and harassment. The purpose was to hurt the manufacturers financially. Working conditions slowly improved when manufacturers realized it was in their best interests to sit down and talk with union leaders to resolve such problems.

The world was quickly changing. The 1880s were a time of mass immigration by millions of newcomers to America. While some came for economic opportunities, others experienced religious and political persecution in Europe and now faced poverty and harsh working conditions in America. Many brought with them varying socialist ideas that they hoped could improve their lives. While most socialists advocated nonviolence, others called for revolution and civil unrest to bring about change. Anarchists promoted the use of violence to achieve their goals.

They all competed for the support of workers both in and out of unions. In Sam's view, their theories would not lead to better working conditions. He opposed socialism and strongly believed that unions must devote their energies to improving workers' lives and not be connected to specific political parties or ideas. To succeed, unions had to focus only on what he called trade unionism or bread-and-butter unionism—wages, working conditions, and hours worked—and not on what he considered unrealistic, radical political ideas.

Cigar Makers' International Union of America Local 144 could not escape the political conflict. A faction of socialist members, unhappy with the leadership of Sam and Strasser, left and formed a competing organization, the Cigar Makers' Progressive Union, allied with the Knights of Labor, which welcomed both skilled and unskilled workers. Sam was disheartened

The Great Railroad Strike of 1877 was not peaceful. Police and workers clashed, strikers burned or destroyed railroad property, and rioters tore up railroad tracks and marched to demonstrate their anger with railroad company management.

by this break in unity. The new group eventually failed when it lowered dues and then could not support its members' needs.

Between work and union activity, Sam spent little time at home. He was not interested in wealth, only in making enough money to keep his growing family fed and safe, and he felt secure knowing he had Sophia's complete support. Often alone and with little money, Sophia unselfishly took care of their home and young children. (Their last child, Sadie, was born in 1883.) Once, during his period of unemployment after the 1877 strike, Sophia told him that a family friend had offered her $30 a week for three months if she would persuade Sam to leave the union. "Well, what did you tell him?" Sam asked. Sophia responded, "What do you suppose I said to him with one child dying and another coming? Of course I took the money." Before a stunned Sam could respond, Sophia added, "Good God, Sam, how could you ask such a question? Don't you know I resented the insult?"

While Sam busied himself with the union, he had a larger dream: to unite with craft workers in other industries in order to create a national union organization. He realized that strength in numbers made a difference and that the struggle for workers' rights could succeed only by bringing all trade unions into one big nationwide organization that spoke with one voice. Several earlier attempts, such as the National Labor Union, met with

failure when they could not concentrate only on workers' issues. But now, after the economic depression of the 1870s, America experienced the growth of large factories powered by steam and electricity. Unskilled workers operated machines that produced everything from tools to typewriters. While mass production lowered prices, skilled workers feared that mechanization threatened their jobs. For Sam, it seemed the right time for workers in various trades to unite. Union leaders in other industries had similar thoughts and called for a national labor congress to take place in Pittsburgh, Pennsylvania, in November 1881.

Sam and Adolph Strasser were two of the representatives of the Cigar Makers' International Union of America at the meeting. By the time Sam arrived in Pittsburgh, he was already known for "his distinctive idealism and earthiness, his spirit of cooperation and individualism, and his self-denial and power-hunger."

After several days of deliberation, 108 delegates representing nearly 200,000 workers from unions and Knights of Labor groups nationwide created a new organization. They named it the Federation of Organized Trades and Labor Unions of the United States and Canada (FOTLU). Despite the grand title, the group was only a loose collection of member unions, each of which maintained its independence. The FOTLU had no central decision-making authority, no full-time leadership, and,

The fight between labor and big business in 1883 is shown as a jousting tournament. A haggard-looking worker on an exhausted horse fights an oversized, well-protected, powerful knight (big business).

most important of all, no money to function. There were no set dues; member unions made voluntary contributions to keep the new federation alive.

Sam was named chairman of the Committee on Organization. This suited him, as it made him responsible for creating the federation's organizational plan. One stumbling block was the Knights of Labor, which Sam accused of not caring enough about the problems of skilled workers. There was a deep rift between Sam and Terence V. Powderly, the Knights' leader. Both men were highly opinionated. Powderly did not believe in strikes. He put his hopes in arbitration and boycotts to solve problems. Sam thought strikes could be effective in the right circumstances. The two men not only differed in their beliefs but personally as well. Powderly was always well dressed. Sam on the other hand was so busy with work and union activities that he paid little attention to his appearance. Although Powderly never drank alcohol, Sam enjoyed beer and socializing in saloons with his union friends.

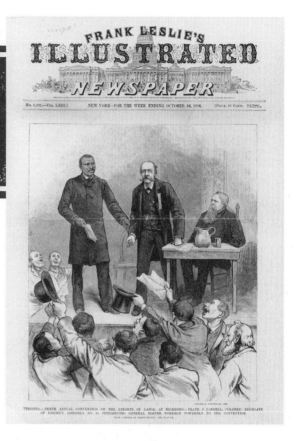

Using his persuasive skills, Sam set out to restrict the Knights' role within the FOTLU. He successfully led his committee to rule that the number of each trade union's voting delegates in the federation would be proportional to its membership size. Non–trade union groups like the Knights would have only one delegate each, thereby blunting their power.

In 1884, Sam was elected one of three FOTLU vice presidents. A year later, at the age of thirty-five, he was elected president. Like the other officers, Sam received no pay. He later recalled, "I worked and supported my family at my trade as cigarmaker. Evenings and holidays and half days off I devoted to work of organization."

The platform adopted by the federation's members clearly stated its immediate goals. First, it urged legal restrictions on future immigration to the United States. American workers feared that unskilled newcomers would take away the jobs of established trade union members. Second, the FOTLU led the fight for a uniform eight-hour workday throughout the country. Third, it called for strict limits on the use of child and convict labor, which the delegates feared could replace union workers. Fourth, the federation wanted workers' wages to be paid in cash. This would eliminate the practice of paying workers with credit slips that could be redeemed only at high-priced company stores.

On May 1, 1886, in cities all over America, local labor unions affiliated with the FOTLU held parades and demonstrations to raise public support for the eight-hour workday. Banners proclaimed, "We will fight for eight hours." Perhaps the largest turnout in the country was in Chicago, where

an estimated 80,000 people marched. There, union workers at the McCormick Harvesting Machine Company were involved in a bitter strike for an eight-hour day. Passions were running high, and on May 3 a violent confrontation broke out on the picket line at the factory, and police shot several strikers. The workers, enraged by the violence, scheduled a mass meeting for the following evening in Haymarket Square to protest the actions of the police.

A crowd of about 2,500 gathered in the square. A vocal group of anarchists put themselves at the demonstration's forefront to create turmoil. As the meeting drew to a close and began to break up, rifle-toting Chicago police officers suddenly moved

In May 1886, during a workers' rally in Chicago's Haymarket Square, a dynamite bomb thrown by anarchists killed eleven people and injured many more. This event led to a setback for unions, which were blamed for the violence.

in to disperse the remaining crowd. Shots erupted from both sides. Without warning, someone in the crowd flung a dynamite bomb that killed seven police officers and four others. This event soon became known as the Haymarket riot.

Police quickly rounded up many known anarchists in the city, most of whom were not at the scene, and charged them with conspiracy and murder. Since many of them were foreign-born, anti-immigrant feelings grew. Eight anarchists were put on trial and found guilty. Seven men were sentenced to death and one man to fifteen years in prison. Of the seven, four were executed, one committed suicide, and two were later pardoned by the governor. One of the condemned men also happened to be a member of the Knights of Labor. The Knights' membership dropped as people incorrectly associated them with the violence.

Although the FOTLU's campaign for the eight-hour day had nothing to do with the violence, organized labor's reputation suffered after the Haymarket riot. Whether they were guilty or not, Sam decided that the condemned anarchists deserved fair treatment. He took a train to Springfield, Illinois, and urged the governor to grant clemency to the prisoners. Sam's appeal failed, and the men were executed.

The FOTLU was an organization without any real power. Decision making and action were limited by an unreliable treasury, Knights of Labor members, and part-time officers. Sam supported transforming the FOTLU into a stronger national federation of skilled workers without ties to the Knights. The new group would focus only on improving wages and working conditions for skilled workers. At a convention held in November 1886 in Columbus, Ohio, the FOTLU reorganized itself as the American Federation of Labor (AFL), "a consolidated organization for the promotion of trade unionism." For

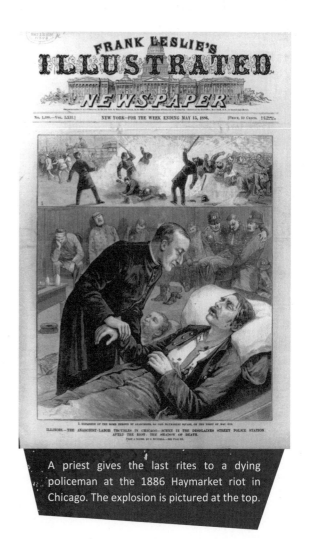

A priest gives the last rites to a dying policeman at the 1886 Haymarket riot in Chicago. The explosion is pictured at the top.

its official seal, Sam thought back to the Hand-in-Hand Society and its logo of two hands clasping, and he inserted it over the image of a globe. The message was clear: the AFL stood for unity and cooperation for all American workers.

As in the FOTLU, each member union maintained its own leadership and ability to address its unique needs. But, recognizing the need for responsible leadership, the new federation created an executive committee of elected officers to make timely decisions between conventions. Sam was elected president and instituted a required-dues system to ensure a steady flow of funds. At first he refused to accept any pay, but the organizers insisted on a full-time, paid leader. The salary of $1,000 a year was the first money Sam ever received for union work.

For the Gompers family, this job presented a challenge. Sam could make more money as a working cigar maker, but he waited until March 1887 for his FOTLU contract and salary as president to take effect. The family understood the situation and, Sam later recalled, "simply did the best we could." He knew he could rely on the continued support of his wife and children. They were used to hardships at home.

Even when Sam began to receive his salary, he spent most of it on union needs, often traveling to cities across the country to build union membership. The AFL could not afford to pay for all his travel expenses, so he often paid for his train tickets out of his own pocket. "Many a time the children had to stay home while shoes or clothes were repaired—there were no changes," he later remembered. "Many a night the children went to bed hungry."

The AFL "needed a central office and officers who could give all their time to the Federation work." The organization's first headquarters was in a small shed in New York City that Sam borrowed from Cigar Makers' International Union Local 144. It was cold in winter and hot in summer. The desk was Sam's old kitchen table. Wooden tomato crates donated by a neighboring grocer served as filing cabinets. Sam's twelve-year-old son, Henry, became the part-time office boy, working after school for $3 a week. Sometimes there was money to pay him, but often not. When there was no money for paper and ink, Henry borrowed supplies from the nearby public school. To save money, Sam walked the three miles from his home to the office in all kinds of weather. Such was the humble beginning of America's most powerful labor union.

FOUR
"WHAT DOES LABOR WANT?"

"We want more schoolhouses and less jails; more books and less arsenals; more learning and less vice; more leisure and less greed."
—Samuel Gompers

The early years of the American Federation of Labor were filled with challenges, but Sam was ready for them. From his past experiences, he understood that to succeed, the new organization needed "a stable membership, a well-filled treasury, a rational strike policy, centralized control, and discipline." His immediate job was to grow union membership, keep peace among all the member unions, and serve as the public voice for unionism. From the beginning, he set out to build a strong union that could make a difference in workers' lives. It would not be easy.

The AFL's organization reflected Sam's strong belief in democracy. With limited powers as president, he reported to an executive committee composed of the union's elected officers, who could approve or reject his actions. Ultimate decision making rested in an annual convention at which elected delegates from all the member unions assembled to debate and vote on union affairs. But Sam was never shy about using his

Samuel Gompers in 1886, at the age of thirty-six

Frank Morrison of the International Typographical Union, and James Duncan of the Granite Cutters' National (later International) Union.

Most Americans knew nothing about the American Federation of Labor, so Sam took steps to publicize its existence. First, he urged all member unions to proudly proclaim their affiliation with the AFL on their letterheads and in their publications. Second, he received permission to publish a journal called the *Trade Union Advocate*. Sam thought of the journal as a way to keep in touch with union members across the country and provide them with information and news about union activities. Sam was the editor and main writer, while his son Henry, his office boy, helped fold and address the copies by hand. A year later, after just seven issues and against Sam's wishes, the annual convention voted to discontinue the journal for lack of interest and because of the cost of publication.

Sam's first years in office kept him away from home for weeks on end as he traveled around the country. His main job was to attract members to the new federation. To secure them, Sam thought it was important to establish personal contact with as many workers as possible. No group was too small or too far away for him to visit. He enjoyed meeting people and making friends who might be helpful to the cause in the future. Many times, his success in winning over new union members relied on his ability

speaking skills and powers of persuasion to try to get his way. Sam was more than just a good speaker; he was also an executive and a general. He had "learned the secret of leadership, that of gathering about him trusty lieutenants and leaving to them the details." He explained, "The best leaders issue always the fewest orders. They surround themselves with subordinates they can trust."

From the beginning, Sam received the loyal support and friendship of Executive Committee members who became close advisers. They included Peter J. McGuire of the Brotherhood of Carpenters and Joiners of America, John B. Lennon of the Journeymen Tailors' Union of America, to connect with workers, often with a beer in his hand. He became an accomplished speaker but usually went hungry at dinner meetings because he refused to eat before giving a speech.

He was in constant motion, all the while taking care of routine union business. In December 1889, he set out on a long trip through forty cities mainly in the Midwest, speaking to union groups and business owners. Everywhere he went, he contacted newspaper reporters to drum up publicity for the union. He appeared before a legislative committee in Indiana, and he testified on behalf of the eight-hour workday before the House of Representatives' Committee on Labor in Washington, DC. Sam was now a nationally known figure, quoted frequently in newspapers and widely recognized as the voice of American workers. He was outspoken in his support for the eight-hour day, telling one reporter, "The eight hour day is coming. . . . It is gathering momentum every day and every hour."

By the time he returned to New York in March 1890, he had succeeded in organizing unions in a wide variety of occupations, from brewery workers and meatcutters to musicians and garment workers. He lamented that he had to pay $90 out of his $1,000 yearly salary to cover travel expenses, but he knew the AFL had little money to work with in those early years. "Our Federation was poor," Sam later remembered. "The organizations were poor. The wage-earners were poor."

Although Sam thrived on the travel and speaking, this was a trying time for Sophia and the children. Their oldest son, Samuel, like his father years earlier, left school to help support the family. They moved frequently, and often their rented

In this humorous cartoon, a man demonstrates for the eight-hour day, while housewives in the background also demonstrate for a shorter workday.

homes lacked running water. The toilet was often in the backyard, and a hydrant would provide the family with drinking water. Time and again, Sophia turned to the Hand-in-Hand Society for aid. Ever proud, she kept covered pots filled with water simmering on the stove so visitors would think there was food in the house. Despite the poverty and Sam's long absences, the family was happy. Sam fondly recalled that when they lived on Sixty-Ninth Street—their first home with running water and indoor plumbing—he enjoyed taking his sons to nearby Jones' Wood to picnic and play ball.

In 1888, the front room in their small three-room apartment on Ninety-First Street became the AFL headquarters. Sam kept copies of every letter and article and never threw anything away, and soon the files and boxes overwhelmed the family. Sophia and the children also had little privacy, as Sam received visitors at all hours. To keep peace in the family, Sam agreed to move the AFL headquarters to a three-room rented office at 16 Clinton Place, downtown.

As membership numbers grew, so did the AFL treasury. No longer dependent on voluntary payments from member unions, the AFL required each individual member to pay dues of one and a half cents per month. The pennies added up, allowing Sam to expand the AFL's work and receive payment for his travel and office expenses. Life became a bit more comfortable for the Gompers family as his salary slowly increased.

At a time when unions were quick to go on strike, Sam urged caution, especially in situations where the workers couldn't expect to win. "The stronger the union the fewer the strikes," he said. "We are opposed to sympathetic and foolish strikes." Strikes—even unsuccessful ones (and most were)—required adequate funds to support workers and their families. Sam preferred to pursue negotiations with employers to settle problems. And if a strike was unavoidable, he urged member unions to "strengthen your position so that you may have a good chance of victory before you strike." Not all unions followed his advice, however, and two violent, historic strikes proved his point and hurt the labor movement's image.

In Homestead, Pennsylvania, just across the Monongahela River from Pittsburgh, lay the massive Homestead Works. Owned by the Carnegie Steel Company, the mill was one of the largest in the world, producing steel for buildings and bridges. It employed thousands of workers. Work in the mill was hard and dangerous; workers could be burned by molten iron or crushed by heavy machinery. While they worked, poisonous gases and intense heat surrounded them. But workers accepted those risks. Thanks to their membership in the Amalgamated Association of Iron and Steel Workers (AA), a founding union of the AFL, they had better working conditions and wages than many other steelworkers.

By June 1892, however, the price of steel had dropped sharply due to innovations in technology. The mill required fewer skilled workers to produce even more steel. With the current union contract about to expire and with the approval of company owner Andrew Carnegie, the plant manager, Henry Clay Frick, set out to remove the union and impose lower wages and increased hours on the workers. Sam urged caution, but when Frick refused to negotiate, the union called a strike.

Frick erected a twelve-foot-high wooden fence topped with barbed wire around the plant to lock out current workers. He then sent out a call for replacement nonunion workers, particularly new immigrants who would work for lower wages. Sam advised union organizers to keep strikebreakers away from the mill and alerted unions in other cities to discourage immigrant strikebreakers from traveling to Homestead. With angry union picketers mobilizing and threatening violence, Frick quietly hired three hundred Pinkerton agents to guard the property and allow replacement workers to enter the factory grounds. (The Pinkerton National Detective Agency was a private security guard and detective agency founded in 1850 to provide services to business and government clients.)

Getting the agents to the property was a problem because union protesters guarded the roads into Homestead. In the early morning hours of July 6, 1892, two barges loaded with rifle-carrying Pinkertons made their way silently up the Monongahela River toward the mill. Union lookouts quickly caught sight of the approaching vessels and sounded

FRANK LESLIE'S
ILLUSTRATED
HOMESTEAD TROUBLES.
WEEKLY

NEW YORK, JULY 14, 1892.

THE LABOR TROUBLES AT HOMESTEAD, PENNSYLVANIA—ATTACK OF THE STRIKERS AND THEIR SYMPATHIZERS ON THE SURRENDERED PINKERTON MEN.

Pinkerton detectives were attacked by strikers and their families at the Carnegie steel mill in Homestead, Pennsylvania, on July 6, 1892. The workers won the battle but lost the strike.

The Pennsylvania National Guard arrives at the Carnegie Company in Homestead, Pennsylvania, on July 12, 1892.

the alarm. Awakened by prearranged blasts of a steam whistle, workers and their families rushed from their homes, some carrying guns and clubs. They reached the river as the first group of Pinkertons stepped ashore. Shots rang out from both sides, and the Pinkertons quickly retreated to the barges.

The strikers tried to burn the barges by setting the river on fire and tossing in sticks of dynamite. In a battle that lasted eight hours, seven strikers and three Pinkerton agents died and over thirty were severely wounded. The surviving Pinkertons, who feared for their lives and were unable to escape, had no choice but to surrender. Armed strikers marched them through threatening crowds and put them on a train out of town. The next day, grisly newspaper reports of the battle shocked the nation. The governor ordered 8,000 members of the Pennsylvania National Guard to guard the plant and maintain order.

Although the union workers won the battle, they lost the war. The public blamed the workers for the violence and turned against them even more when an anarchist named Alexander Berkman, who had no connection to the strikers, shot Frick. He was only wounded and within days continued with his antiunion plans. In August, Sam traveled to Homestead to assure the strikers of his support and to promise financial help, but it was too late. Strike leaders were arrested and, though later cleared by a jury, were never again hired to work in a steel mill. The plant reopened with nonunion replacement workers, including new immigrants from eastern Europe. The workers' salaries were drastically cut, and they were required to work twelve hours a day, six days a week.

For Sam, working hard to establish a positive image for labor, the tragedy of Homestead was followed by an even larger disappointment.

The community of Pullman, Illinois, just outside Chicago, seemed the ideal place to live and work. Neat, well-cared-for employee houses lined the streets around the Pullman's Palace Car Company factory; banks, shops, schools, and a theater were within walking distance. This was a model city, and George Pullman owned it all. Pullman's invention of a railroad car with sleeping berths had revolutionized long-distance rail travel. Railroads bought and attached Pullman cars to their trains,

offering passengers a comfortable way to travel. The cars made George Pullman wealthy.

In 1893, America entered another economic depression. Unemployment rose dramatically, and companies went bankrupt, including a number of railroads. Sales of Pullman cars dropped. Pullman cut workers' wages dramatically and at the same time refused to lower the rents on their homes. Outraged workers, now unable to provide adequately for their families, turned to the American Railway Union (ARU)—not an AFL member—for help. When they declared a strike against the company in May 1894, Pullman closed the factory.

In response, ARU members refused to move any train carrying a Pullman car, paralyzing rail traffic throughout the country. Violence on the picket lines escalated as angry workers destroyed railroad equipment, including hundreds of railcars. Shipments of fresh produce and manufactured goods stopped. By early July 1894, the strike was affecting the entire American economy. President Grover Cleveland had to act, but he couldn't legally interfere in a private industry. He needed an excuse for the federal government to intervene.

He found it when he realized that the railroads carried United States mail. "If it takes the entire army and navy of the United States to deliver a postal card into Chicago,"

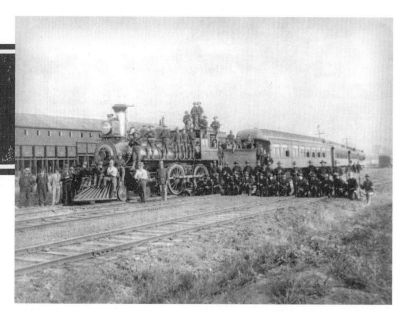

Soldiers from Company C of the 15th United States Infantry protect the Rock Island Railroad line at Blue Island, Illinois, from strikers during the Pullman Railroad Strike in 1894.

Cleveland forcefully declared, "that postal card will be delivered." The government obtained a court order (called an injunction) against the workers to immediately halt their strike. When the workers refused to return to their jobs, the president ordered 14,000 federal troops and United States marshals into action. Together with local police, they slowly took control, reducing the violence and vandalism, but not before one incident horrified the nation.

In Chicago, where railroad strikers were especially active, troops fired into a crowd of 10,000 protesters, killing twenty-five and wounding over sixty. Hundreds more were arrested, including ARU leaders. Eugene V. Debs, head of the railway union, called on Sam and the American Federation of Labor to join the fight and declare a general strike of all unions throughout the country. Sam traveled to Chicago to meet with railway

union leaders but rejected their pleas for national assistance. He believed that their strike could not succeed and that a general strike of all unions would only drag the AFL into a lost cause. The AFL made a symbolic contribution of $500 to support the strikers but refused to go any further. Ultimately, the Pullman workers and their railway union supporters had no choice but to return to their jobs. Their failed effort influenced other employers to use injunctions against labor unions, a tactic that the United States Supreme Court upheld in 1895.

The strike presented a dilemma to President Cleveland. Although he felt there was no choice but to intervene, he also knew there was an election coming up, and he wanted the union workers' votes. To curry favor with the unions, on June 28, 1894, the president signed a congressional bill proclaiming the first Monday in September a national holiday, Labor Day. In many European countries, a workers' holiday was celebrated on May 1. But because that day was associated with anarchists, socialists, and violent revolutionaries, American labor leaders favored September. Indeed, Sam had long advocated for such a holiday to be observed in September. "Labor Day," he once said, "differs in every essential from other holidays of the year in any country. . . . Labor Day is devoted to no man, living or dead, to no sect, race or nation."

In fact, the unofficial observance of this holiday had begun in 1882, when workers in New York City started celebrating a yearly holiday called Labor Day in their honor. Other states adopted the observance, but it did not become a national holiday until 1894. After signing the bill into law, President Cleveland, recognizing the role Sam and the AFL played in the fight for the eight-hour workday and other workers' rights, sent the pen he used to Sam.

Sam turned his attention to building the union. For years, he had complained about the lack of a national union journal

Union bakers proudly carry a very large loaf of bread during the 1909 Labor Day parade in New York City.

to replace the old *Trade Union Advocate*. Finally, the delegates to the 1893 AFL convention voted to establish the *American Federationist*. Sam was again named editor, and in his first editorial in March 1894, he wrote that the journal's purpose was "to voice the demands of the toiling masses, to advocate their rights, to expose the wrongs from which they suffer." Sam devoted much time and energy to writing for and editing the *American Federationist*. To him, it was the best way to keep in touch with union members across the country.

With the nation in the grip of an economic depression, socialist members of the AFL tried to push the union into a strong political stand. At the 1893 annual convention, they introduced a resolution calling for "collective ownership by the people of all means of production and distribution." Known as Plank 10, the resolution met with Sam's opposition. "I am entirely at variance with your philosophy," he told socialists. "Economically, you are unsound; socially, you are wrong; industrially, you are an impossibility."

Sam used his political skills to defeat Plank 10 in 1893 and again the following year. His rejection of the plank angered socialists. At the 1894 AFL convention, they joined with others who differed with Sam's beliefs and leadership style to vote him out of office and elect John McBride of the United Mine Workers of America as president instead. The vote was close—1,170 to 976.

The delegates also voted to move AFL headquarters from New York to Indianapolis, Indiana. Sam politely accepted their decision but later snippily told a group of New York socialists, "After killing me and nicely laying me away, you find I still live." Perhaps feeling somewhat guilty at ousting their founding president, the AFL elected him as one of two delegates to the British Trades Union Congress.

With the weight of leadership lifted, Sam found himself surprisingly energized. But he quickly returned to the reality of being forty-five years old, without any savings, and out of a job. He first thought about returning to work as a cigar maker but found he could support his family in a more productive way. By then, Sam had become an accomplished speaker. He drew on that skill to accept well-paying speaking engagements across the country, which for the first time greatly improved his family's finances.

But he could not ignore his commitment to labor. He traveled through the South to organize workers for the United Garment Workers of America. "That trip constituted my first real acquaintance with the South," he recalled. "It brought me face to face with facts which no intelligent person could ignore." Although he supported African American workers' right to equality in their jobs, he was skeptical about the idea of black and white social equality. Reflecting the pervading beliefs of the time, he said, "That southern trip made me realize the difference between racial problems as theories and practical situations."

The best part of that year for Sam was having time to participate in family affairs as husband and father. On July 29, 1895, however, Sam was in a police court defending his son, Alexander. The seventeen-year-old had been arrested for illegally playing baseball in the street on Sunday. Alexander told the court that the police officer had knocked him down. Sam was angry and threatened to bring a complaint against the officer. The judge let the boy go free with no punishment.

On August 14, Sam and Peter J. McGuire, the first vice president of the AFL, boarded the steamship *Berlin* bound for England and the British Trades Union Congress in Cardiff, Wales. A delegation of AFL leaders and a brass band saw them off. Both men received a warm reception at the congress, where Sam proudly told the delegates that their organization and the AFL could be compared to the British Parliament and the United States Congress. Sam and McGuire received special medals commemorating their visit, and the entire British Trades Union Congress serenaded them with "For They Are Jolly Good Fellows."

This was Sam's first time back in England since he left in 1863, and he took special pleasure in revisiting the London neighborhood of his childhood. From there, he and McGuire were off on a whirlwind trip to Manchester, Liverpool,

Dublin, Paris, Cologne, Bremen, Antwerp, Hamburg, and Amsterdam. In each city, Sam spoke with workers and labor leaders. He also took time to visit members of the extended Gompers family. On September 21, the two men boarded the steamer *New York* to return home.

The year passed quickly. During that time, through speeches, newspaper articles, and interviews, Sam was often in the public eye. When the 1895 AFL convention opened in New York in December, Sam was elected president over John McBride by the narrow vote of 1,041 to 1,023. He never lost another election.

Sam left his family behind in New York and went to Indianapolis to take charge of the AFL. There he found a disorganized mess. He worked long hours to straighten out the office and organize the past year's worth of documents and correspondence. As a result, he became seriously ill. For two weeks, he suffered in pain, confined to bed, until Sophia arrived from New York to nurse him back to health. When he was recovered, she returned to New York.

Sam increased the size of the office staff and set up a businesslike system for record keeping. Once he knew that the office was in good hands, he resumed a busy travel schedule. He was now the undisputed leader of American workers. One newspaper commented, "Samuel Gompers is one of the ablest men in the ranks of labor. He is considered conservative and earnest. His speeches are terse statements of conditions and carefully prepared." Sam made the union respectable and built an impressive image for himself as Mr. Labor.

More and more, Sam realized that the most practical way to achieve labor success was through legislative and judicial means. Indianapolis was a central location but not a center of political power. At the 1896 AFL convention, the delegates voted to move the organization's headquarters to Washington, DC. Sam understood that having the headquarters in the nation's capital symbolized the AFL's growing importance in American life.

FIVE
STRUGGLES AND CHALLENGES

"Stand faithfully by our friends, oppose and defeat our enemies."

—Samuel Gompers

When Sam relocated the AFL headquarters to Washington, DC, in 1897, he moved his family there as well. The new headquarters at first occupied three rooms of an office building at Fourteenth and G Streets NW. As the organization grew, the headquarters moved to the Typographical Temple, a union hall on G Street NW, and then to three floors in the Ouray Building, on the same street. The Gompers family—including adult children Henry, a stonecutter; Alexander, a cigar maker; and Sadie—first moved into a small, six-room home on H Street NE. When Alexander married, the family moved to a larger home on First Street NW. In 1891, Rose had married Samuel Mitchell, a postal worker, and they lived in New York City. The other Gompers children were on their own. Abe worked in the clothing industry in New York, while Samuel lived in Washington and worked for the Government Printing Office. Except for Sadie, they were all union members.

Sam was now in the center of American political power but still believed that the AFL needed to remain neutral in supporting candidates or political parties. Those choices, he thought, belonged to union members individually. He did have his own opinions, and though not reluctant to publicize them, he drew the line at endorsing candidates. During the 1896 presidential campaign, many union members favored Democrat William Jennings Bryan over Republican William McKinley. Bryan supported workers' rights. McKinley represented the business community. Sam agreed with Bryan's famous campaign slogan, "You shall not crucify mankind upon a cross of gold," but he refused to publicly endorse him.

While steering clear of politics, Sam did not hesitate to tackle controversial issues facing the AFL. From early in his union work, Sam had sought to combat discrimination against African Americans within national union affairs.

Some unaffiliated unions had clauses in their constitutions banning African Americans. When these unions applied for AFL membership, Sam refused to accept them unless they removed the offending words. But some unions, even after joining the AFL, continued to discriminate unofficially. To keep peace within the AFL, and recognizing that Americans were still divided by race, Sam did not criticize them too loudly.

Sam saw his responsibility as AFL president as first and foremost to protect American workers. That's why he opposed mass immigration to the United States. "Some way must be found to safeguard America," he said. Though an immigrant himself, he believed strongly that the masses of Italians, Jews, Poles, and Greeks coming into the country at the beginning

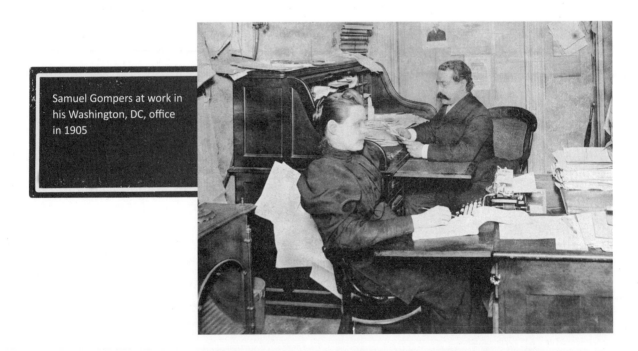

Samuel Gompers at work in his Washington, DC, office in 1905

of the twentieth century threatened Americans' livelihoods.

He particularly opposed the employment of Chinese immigrants in the West Coast cigar industry. Earlier, Sam had supported passage of the Chinese Exclusion Act of 1882, which temporarily limited Chinese immigration and prohibited those already here from becoming United States citizens. Although he stated, "I have no prejudice against the Chinese people," he vigorously fought Chinese immigration at a time of active discrimination against the Chinese in America. Sam would later back the successful fight in Congress that made Chinese exclusion permanent in 1902.

Despite his strong views on immigration to the United States, Sam supported workers' rights and union activity in other countries. In the mid-1890s, American attention was focused on the Caribbean island of Cuba, where a revolution against Spanish rule was in progress. Public opinion in the United States, influenced by lurid newspaper stories of Spanish cruelty and Cuban suffering, favored an American war against Spain.

Sam met with José Martí and other Cuban revolutionary leaders in New York and supported their quest for freedom. He was particularly concerned about protecting the island's respected cigar makers. In a speech at New York's Cooper Union on March 11, 1897, Sam spoke up for workers but against going to war: "At best the profession of militarism is the profession of slaughter. At best it is barbaric." Then, to much applause, he declared, "Upon the masses of labor . . . has always fallen the burden of war, to furnish the sinews of war while war lasts, to bear the burdens of increased taxation when war has ended, and to be shot to death upon the battle-field while war is in progress."

On February 15, 1898, a mysterious explosion destroyed the United States warship *Maine* in Havana harbor. Calls of "Remember the Maine!" echoed throughout the country, leading the United States to declare war on Spain. Spanish forces were no match for American military might, which within the year drove Spain from the Americas and the Philippine Islands in the Pacific. Secretary of State John Hay summed up American feelings about the Spanish-American War when he wrote, "It has been a splendid little war."

Even while speaking out against the war, Sam was "glad of aid for the Cuban revolutionaries, but . . . very apprehensive lest the United States inaugurate a régime of imperialism." He opposed American occupation of other countries and became an active leader of the American Anti-Imperialist League. Two years after the war, Sam traveled to Cuba to participate in a memorial ceremony for the sinking of the *Maine*. During that trip and others that followed, he met with labor union members and visited cigar factories to promote the growth of unionism in Cuba.

At the end of the war, the United States found itself in possession of the Philippine Islands, which Sam opposed. "We cannot annex the Philippines," Sam said, "without a large increase in our standing army. . . . We shall have to conquer the Filipinos by force of arms, and thereby deny to them what we claim to ourselves—the right to self-government." In an October 18, 1898 speech, Sam described his anti-immigration feelings crudely. "If the Philippines are annexed what is to prevent the Chinese, the Negritos and Malays coming to our country? How can we prevent the Chinese coolies from going to the Philippines and from there swarm into the United States and engulf our people and our civilization?"

Sam's focus on union work was sometimes interrupted by unexpected events. During a trip to Iowa in 1898, Sam was in the middle of a speech when someone put a telegram in front of him. He glanced at it while continuing to talk and then suddenly stopped. His married daughter, Rose Gompers Mitchell, was dead. "I tried to finish my talk but could not," he later recalled. Sam caught the first train to New York to attend her funeral. Rose left behind two young daughters, whom Sam and Sophia took into their household until their father remarried. Within two days of the funeral, Sam was back on a train, continuing his speaking tour.

A year later, on December 6, 1899, Sam hurried from New York to Washington for a meeting with President William McKinley. After spending a few minutes with his wife and family, he hopped on his bicycle for the short trip to the White House. Within moments, he crashed into a passing streetcar and was severely injured. Neighbors carried him back to his house, where doctors treated him for a punctured lung and broken ribs. He was under orders not to move from his bed. One newspaper reported, "He cannot speak save in monosyllables, and every effort to do even this much causes him excruciating pain."

The AFL convention was due to open in Detroit later that month, and Sam could not stay away. Disregarding the doctors, he enlisted a union friend, John Morrison, to accompany him to Detroit by train. Sam's feet were so swollen he couldn't wear shoes. He put on a pair of rubber-lined boots and hobbled along with the aid of crutches. After speaking slowly and in pain to the delegates, he retired to his hotel room and recuperated there for a week.

In 1900, Sam helped create the National Civic Federation (NCF) to bring together business and union leaders to discuss and peacefully resolve labor disputes. It included an influential group of nationally known industrialists, railroad owners, bankers, and key union leaders, including Sam's friends and AFL officers John Mitchell of the United Mine Workers of America and James Duncan of the Granite Cutters' National Union. The members elected Sam vice president.

For Sam, this was an opportunity to meet on common ground with business leaders who otherwise would never interact socially with him. Sam used this association to make businesspeople realize that there was a labor problem. To achieve progress in legislation favored by unions, it couldn't hurt to have business friends. Some AFL leaders viewed with suspicion Sam's membership in a group that included wealthy antilabor people. But he realized that membership in the NCF opened avenues of communication that benefited workers. He humorously told his AFL associates that although he never ate at the fancy NCF banquets, he also never refused the offer of a good cigar.

In the past, Sam had always enjoyed the secret rituals, ceremonies, and friendships of fraternal groups, and now he became interested in the Freemasons, the world's oldest fraternity. He was drawn into the worldwide organization, which emphasized self-improvement, fellowship, and philanthropy. He joined Dawson Lodge #16 in Washington and appreciated being in a group where discussions about politics were forbidden. During his travels in the United States and Europe, he often found time to attend local Masonic lodge meetings.

On July 27, 1901, Sam had a second mishap with a Washington streetcar. Returning home from a picnic with his daughter, Sadie, and granddaughter Florence, Sam stepped off the streetcar just as it unexpectedly lurched forward. He toppled onto the street, and his head struck the pavement. Unconscious, the fifty-one-year-old was carried to his house, and a doctor was called. The *New York Times* reported, "There is only a slight chance of his recovery." But the *Washington Times* noted that, according to his doctor, "there is no occasion to fear for his life. The patient has an excellent constitution and great recuperative powers." Sam was back at work within a few days.

That year, Sam reconnected with Theodore Roosevelt, now president, whose association with Sam went back to the New York State Legislature and the fight against tenement shops. Sam wrote, "Time and time again, Roosevelt had me at the White House from seven o'clock on—he with his tennis clothes on, and me without dinner." Sam never let politeness, even toward a president, prevent him from standing up for workers. On one occasion, during a heated discussion, Roosevelt hit the desk angrily and said, "Mr. Gompers, I want you to understand, sir, that I am the President of the United States." To which an equally angry Sam, also hitting the desk, responded, "Mr. President, I want you to understand that I am the president of the American Federation of Labor."

Sam's main job up to that time had been to grow the AFL's membership. This he had succeeded in doing. With over 2 million members by 1904—13 percent of all American workers—the AFL was a visible force in American life. But now Sam faced a challenge that affected the very existence of labor unions—the Sherman Antitrust Act, which Congress had passed in 1890.

The act protected consumers from unethical business practices by limiting monopolies and preventing corporations from unfairly interfering with competitors. It called for harsh penalties for violations, with violators subject to paying triple damages. Sam understood the dangers to unions that lurked in the act: "I was convinced that if trade unions were not specifically excluded from the provisions of the measure, the law would be applied to the organized efforts of the workers." The act targeted two tools used by unions to put pressure on employers when negotiations failed—boycotts and strikes. Boycotts convinced consumers not to buy a company's products. If all else failed, workers went on strike.

Since the court injunctions against unions in the Pullman Strike of 1894, Sam and the AFL unions had been under constant legal attack by American manufacturers, who had organized the American Anti-Boycott Association. Business owners successfully turned to the courts to apply antitrust laws to striking workers. Sam found himself at the center of two of the most well-known cases that ultimately reached the United States Supreme Court. They concerned striking hat makers and stove polishers.

In 1902, workers at Loewe & Company in Danbury, Connecticut, tried to unionize the hat-making company. When the owner refused even to meet with union organizers, the workers went on strike. The company then hired replacement workers. The union responded by alerting retailers around the country to the strike and urged them not to carry Loewe & Company hats. When Loewe's name appeared in the We Don't Patronize column of the *American Federationist*, the company went to court. With the assistance of the American Anti-Boycott Association, Loewe filed injunctions against the hatters' union for going on strike

Seal of the American Federation of Labor: The image of two hands in a handshake was taken from the logo of the Hand-in-Hand Society, a mutual aid society that helped poor Jewish immigrant families, including the Gompers family, in New York City.

and against the AFL for advocating the boycott of the company's hats.

The case finally reached the Supreme Court in 1908. In a decision that shocked workers, the Court ruled that the AFL's boycott was illegal according to the Sherman Antitrust Act. The threat to unions was clear. All strikes were now illegal, and unions lost the most important tool they had against business owners. "At the present time, under these conspiracy laws," Sam bitterly complained, "labor organizations seem to be deprived of the chief reasons for their existence."

To add to the punishment, Loewe used a provision in the Sherman Antitrust Act to punish each of the striking workers with triple monetary damages. To save hundreds of hatters from financial ruin, the AFL paid the damages by declaring two national Hatters' Days, on which individual AFL members nationally donated one hour's pay to the hatters. For Sam, this unselfish act was what union membership was all about.

Sam became personally involved in another lawsuit stemming from the Sherman Antitrust Act. In August 1908, union metal polishers at Buck's Stove and Range Company in St. Louis, Missouri, went on strike for a nine-hour workday. When Buck's would not negotiate with the workers, the AFL added the company to the We Don't Patronize list. Buck's went to court and received an injunction against the AFL prohibiting it to list the company.

The AFL appealed, but the company asked the judge to hold Sam and two other union leaders, John Mitchell and Frank Morrison, personally in contempt of court for keeping Buck's on the boycott list. The judge found the men guilty and sentenced them to one year in jail, but released them on bail pending an appeal to a higher court. Union workers across the country defended the men. The Illinois United Mine Workers sent a telegram to President Roosevelt saying, "A law that denies the use of a free press and free speech is a breach of the fundamental principles of our country."

The case was ultimately resolved in 1911 when the company reached a deal with the workers. Although Sam removed the company from the boycott list, he continued to write about the injustice of the court's decision. He explained in the *American Federationist* that the lawsuit has been "an invasion of the liberty of the press and the right of free speech." This led to new charges against Sam, Mitchell, and Morrison for contempt. With a jail sentence hanging over his head, Sam focused more intently on overturning the antitrust laws that stifled union activity.

Sam knew that the unsympathetic courts were only ruling on laws passed by Congress, and he now understood that he needed to move the AFL away from its long-held tradition of noninvolvement in politics and to become politically active. That was the only way to get bad laws changed and new laws favoring unions passed. Up to that time, he and other union members had been free to support the political parties and candidates of their choice. Now, however, the AFL would work as an organization to elect candidates for political office who supported labor and to defeat those who did not.

Sam wrote to a union official in Maine working to oust an antiunion congressman, "Let the slogan go forth that we will stand by our friends and administer a stinging rebuke to men or parties who are either indifferent, negligent, or hostile, and, wherever opportunity affords, to secure the election of intelligent, honest, earnest trade unionists, with clear, unblemished, paid-up union cards in their possession." Sam was leading the AFL into a new political era.

Samuel Gompers, age fifty-two, in 1902

SIX
GAINING RESPECT

"Justice has been done to the laborer."
—President Woodrow Wilson

Sam felt at home in the White House, in the parlor of a fancy hotel, or in a bar having a beer with workers clad in overalls. He was always in the public eye, traveling constantly around the country, addressing local unions, civic organizations, any group, small or large, that might advance labor's cause. He had a powerful voice and prided himself on his speaking abilities.

For Sam, the good life meant being surrounded by people, engaging in good conversation, and enjoying ample amounts of food and drink. Newspapers made fun of his growing girth. Stage comedians got loud laughs by patting their stomachs and calling their own expanded waistlines Sam Gomperses. He projected the image of a gentleman and became very conscious of his appearance. He was not tall, and with his unusually short legs, he appeared to waddle as he walked. But he was built sturdily and dressed well, and he carried a fancy cane in his hand. A good cigar was often between his lips.

Sam's typical speaking schedule found him in constant motion. In Lawrence, Massachusetts, local union members greeted him with a formal reception and then led him in a parade to a packed local theater. After addressing the crowd, he was the guest of honor at a lavish banquet, where he told the attendees, "Laboring men and women have the same right to organize for their own benefit as the big corporations and producers." At Harvard University, Sam gave a two-hour speech, and at Cornell University, he spoke to students taking a labor union course. In New York City, he was the featured speaker at a National Civic Federation banquet.

Despite his popularity, he also had critics. Some felt that Sam was too

Samuel Gompers
at age fifty-five, in 1905

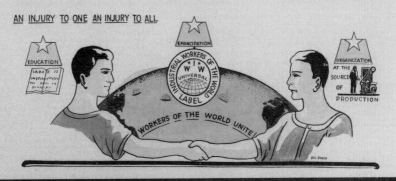

The Industrial Workers of the World (IWW) was founded in 1905 by radical groups that opposed the policies of the AFL. The IWW sought to lead workers toward a revolution to overthrow capitalism.

conservative and too devoted to the American free-enterprise system. Socialist and anarchist members believed that the AFL should work to overthrow the capitalist system, which they saw as being represented by greedy industrialists. At the 1903 AFL convention in Boston, socialist-leaning members introduced a resolution to officially ally the union with socialism. Two years later, a group of socialists founded the Industrial Workers of the World (IWW) as an alternative to the AFL. Called Wobblies, their goal was to create one big union uniting all workers, both skilled and unskilled, to defeat capitalism and create a socialist society. They opposed collective bargaining and advocated violence and sabotage to achieve their goals. To Sam,

"the I.W.W. was frankly revolutionary and had an appeal to a limited number of wage-earners." He called them "rainbow chasers," whose major purpose was to ruin the labor movement. The Wobblies, including their leader, William "Big Bill" Haywood, would be a thorn in Sam's side for years to come.

While Sam fought off his critics, he began to forcefully flex labor's political strength. Sam told a reporter that the AFL "found it necessary . . . , against all its inclinations, to enter into the field of politics in order to try out the matter before the court of public opinion." In 1906, he presented what he called "Labor's Bill of Grievances" to President Theodore Roosevelt and members of Congress. The

59

William "Big Bill" Haywood of the IWW leads strikers in Lowell, Massachusetts, 1912.

document outlined the AFL's demands for improving workers' lives. It called for the enactment of all the policies that Sam and the AFL had long proposed: a national eight-hour workday, the end of prison labor in private industry, restricting immigration, and changing the antitrust and anti-injunction laws that were hurting unions. It ended with a polite threat that if elected officials did not support labor, "we shall appeal to the conscience and the support of our fellow citizens."

In the White House, President Roosevelt

listened to Sam politely but refused to support his demands. In Congress, the powerful Republican Speaker of the House, Joseph "Uncle Joe" Cannon, would not consider anything Sam offered. When

Sam is depicted in this IWW leaflet cover living the good life and socializing with the elite, while William "Big Bill" Haywood of the IWW sits in a jail cell.

These girls are protesting child labor in 1909 by wearing banners saying "Abolish Child Slavery" in English and Yiddish. They are taking part in a labor parade in New York City.

members of Congress friendly to labor tried to introduce pro-labor legislation, the Speaker prevented those bills from coming to a vote. That was as far as labor's legislative activities ever went. Sam complained, "I got hearings, sympathy, and promises, but not labor laws." Popular newspapers took him to task for entangling unions in national politics.

With the presidential election of 1908 looming, Sam appeared before the platform committees of both the Democratic and Republican Parties to appeal for labor support. He received a cold welcome from the Republicans. "We asked for bread," he wrote, "and they showed us a whip." He had better success with the Democrats, who supported the AFL's positions on the eight-hour day and limited use of injunctions. Even with the support of AFL members in the election, Democratic candidates were largely unsuccessful. But the message to elected officials was clear: the AFL, while not officially tied to a political party, was becoming a force too important to ignore.

Sam's continuing work and the lingering

These women on a float represent the Women's Auxilliary Typographical Union in a 1909 Labor Day parade in New York City.

Sophia and Samuel Gompers, both age fifty-eight, in 1908

threat of a jail sentence for contempt charges in the aftermath of the Buck's Stove and Range Company case, took a toll on him physically, which delegates to the 1908 AFL convention recognized. They voted to send him on a four-month trip to Europe in 1909, confident that a change of scenery would help him regain his strength. Union officials insisted that the trip would not be a vacation, knowing that Sam had little patience for sitting still. Instead, aware of his strong feelings about workers' rights around the world, they arranged for him to speak at labor conferences and to confer with European labor leaders. This pleased Sam, as he hoped "to get in closer touch with this international spirit through his trip abroad."

In advance of the trip, union gatherings honored Sam and wished him a safe journey. At one reception, he received a gift of a gold-headed cane, and at another he was given $1,000 for travel expenses. He left for Europe on June 19, accompanied by his wife, Sophia, and his remaining daughter, Sadie. During the trip, he wrote articles about his experiences for American newspapers.

Sam returned to the United States refreshed and ready to continue his work. The reception he received in Washington, DC, on October 12, 1909, was one of the largest ever held in the capital up to that time. A parade featuring bands, floats, and thousands of enthusiastic marchers led Sam to Convention Hall, where he spoke about his trip and, with the appeal of his jail sentence on his mind, about the importance of free speech.

The court of appeals handed down its decision in the case against Sam, John Mitchell, and Frank Morrison on November 3. The court upheld the guilty verdict but reduced the jail sentence. It based its decision solely on the boycott's effect on business while ignoring the free speech issue. With the three men still out on bail, the AFL appealed the decision directly to the United States Supreme Court, arguing that the First Amendment to the Constitution protects free speech and the right to express opinions about a company.

While he nervously awaited the final verdict, several high-profile strikes were receiving national attention. On November 22, 1909, thousands of New York City shirtwaist workers, mostly young immigrant women, gathered to decide whether they should go out on strike. Negotiations with factory owners over low wages and long hours had failed to produce an agreement, and now it was time to act.

Sam was the featured speaker at the event. Speaking in Yiddish to the predominantly Jewish audience, he forcefully told the workers, "I say, friends, do not enter too hastily but when you can't get the manufacturers to give you what you want, then strike. And when you strike, let the manufacturers know you are on strike!" He concluded by urging his listeners "to stand together, to have faith in yourselves, to be true to your comrades. If you strike, be cool, calm, collected and determined. Let your watchword be: Union and progress, and until then no surrender!" The Uprising of the 20,000, as the general strike became known, was the first of several mass strikes that transformed the garment industry. These strikes led to higher salaries and better, though not perfect, working conditions.

Less than two years later, a fire at the Triangle Shirtwaist Company in New

Four women strikers from the Ladies' Tailors' Union walk the picket line during the 1910 "Uprising of the 20,000" garment workers' strike in New York City.

Mass meeting of coal miners on strike in McKees Rocks, Pennsylvania, 1909. When the strike was declared, the workers' families joined together in support.

York City—a nonunion shop—resulted in the deaths of one hundred and fifty-six shirtwaist workers, mostly young Italian and Jewish women immigrants. Sam was horrified by the tragedy and, writing in the *American Federationist*, accused the factory owners of "taking advantage of every means possible to reduce wages and deprive their employes [sic] of the protection of the law or the trade union."

The fire resulted in new laws protecting the safety of workers.

Along with addressing concerns about strikes, legislation, and labor negotiations, Sam wanted to educate the public about unions themselves. For generations of American consumers starting in the 1870s, the union label's appearance on thousands of products indicated that the "people who created the products were fairly treated and

The Stove Mounters' International Union of North America label, 1903

well paid and also that the product was held to the highest standards of quality." The use of union labels began with Sam's cigar makers and quickly spread to other industries. Union products often cost more because union members were usually paid more than nonunion workers. "Every time you buy goods with the label," one advertisement declared, "you strike a blow at unfair manufacturers, sweat-shops and prison workhouses."

Sam's attempts to present unions in a positive way suffered a setback at 1:07 a.m. on October 1, 1910, when a massive explosion ripped through the offices of the *Los Angeles Times*, one of the most important newspapers on the West Coast. The building was destroyed. Twenty-one people died, and dozens more were gravely wounded. The bombing was called the crime of the century. The newspaper was at the time engaged in a bitter fight to keep its employees from unionizing. Suspicion fell almost immediately on the unions, which had been accused of bombing other businesses they had difficulty organizing. Those bombings, targeting property and construction equipment but not people, had served as warnings to employers. This bombing was different.

A group of business owners hired William J. Burns, a well-known private detective, to track down the bombers. Over a period of months, his investigators pieced together a nationwide bombing plot. They discovered that methods and material used in other bombings were identical to those used in Los Angeles. This information led Burns to two brothers in Indianapolis, James B. and

The bombing of the Los Angeles Times Building resulted in twenty-one deaths. The bombers' connection with unions resulted in a decline in public opinion regarding labor unions and their leaders.

John J. McNamara. John was the secretary-treasurer of the International Association of Bridge and Structural Iron Workers, an AFL affiliate. Investigators believed that both brothers and a small circle of union members were connected to other bombings and to the purchase and storing of explosives. John was accused of planning the crime while his brother James actually planted the bomb. In April 1911, Burns secretly bundled John onto a train and delivered him to officials in Los Angeles to stand trial. Union members called it a kidnapping. James was arrested and joined his brother several days later.

Sam was stunned. He and other labor leaders thought the accusations against the McNamara brothers and other union members were nothing more than a plot to "besmirch the name of organized labor." He found it impossible to believe the charges and spoke glowingly of John McNamara as a model citizen and "a painstaking, conscientious, and efficient official." Union leaders charged that the dynamite found in Indianapolis must have been planted by the authorities and that McNamara's arrest was illegal. "How long are the American people going to stand for legalized kidnapping?" Sam asked a reporter.

"The whole thing is a frameup, deep and deep rooted," Sam argued. "I am convinced the accused men are innocent. It is an outrage and the American Federation of Labor shall leave nothing undone in defending the men now imprisoned in Los Angeles. No means

be spared in the matter of counsel for our men." The AFL hired attorney Clarence Darrow to defend the McNamaras, and union members across the country raised money to pay the legal expenses. Darrow was a labor lawyer with experience representing unions. He later became known for defending high-profile clients in criminal cases.

That summer, Sam went to Los Angeles and visited the McNamara brothers in jail. Over and over, John assured Sam of his innocence. "It's all right; you can rely on us," John told him. Looking Sam directly in the eye, he added, "Sam, I want to send a message by you to organized labor and all you may meet. Tell them we're innocent—that we are the victims of an outrageous plot." The meeting convinced Sam even more of the McNamaras' innocence.

Darrow was a good lawyer and realized that the evidence against his clients was powerful. To avoid the death penalty, John McNamara surprised everyone and confessed his guilt. He received a 15-year sentence while James was sentenced to life imprisonment. When he heard the news, Sam broke into tears. "I was horror struck and amazed," he later recalled. Sam proclaimed, "The McNamaras have betrayed labor." Shortly after John's confession, executive officers of major AFL unions sent Sam a telegram informing him of a unanimously adopted motion "declaring their continued confidence in your honesty of purpose and integrity, and expressing the opinion that in your connection with the McNamara case you did only your full duty as the head of the trades union movement on this continent."

Sam went out of his way to try to convince the country that organized labor did not believe in the destruction of property and certainly not in killing people. "What was done was the work of individuals," he told a reporter. "Those who are guilty are guilty as individuals and they do not represent either the iron workers or the spirit of the laboring men."

Despite Sam's disappointment in the McNamaras, the election of 1910 lifted his spirits. Democrats, who were more supportive of workers than Republicans, gained control of the United States House of Representatives. Sam held out hope for the passage of national pro-labor legislation, including the eight-hour workday and an end to punishing antiunion injunctions. The new Democratic Speaker of the House, James Beauchamp "Champ" Clark, pushed several pro-labor bills through the House, but these bills failed because of the opposition of Republican president William Howard Taft and the Republican-controlled Senate. The 1912 election was a welcome turning point. Democrat Woodrow Wilson was elected president, and the Democrats won control of the Senate while maintaining control of the House.

Sam strongly believed in American institutions and took his civic responsibilities seriously. Here, he casts his vote in the 1910 Congressional election.

Streetcars were a key transportation source in American cities. Strikes by streetcar workers often resulted in violent conflicts between unions and police. Here, streetcar strikers in New York City demonstrate their unity in a 1916 parade.

For years, Sam and the AFL had fought to give workers a voice at the highest levels of the American government. On March 4, 1913, just hours before Wilson was inaugurated, President Taft signed into law a bill establishing the United States Department of Labor, a new cabinet-level department. Though not convinced of the need for the department, Taft realized that his successor would create it anyway. American workers now had official government recognition. Sam was particularly delighted that the president appointed as the first secretary of labor William B. Wilson, a former coal miner and a proud union member.

The presidency of Woodrow Wilson invigorated Sam. All the goals he had laid out in his 1906 "Labor's Bill of Grievances" became law. The most appreciated success was the passage, in 1914, of the Clayton Antitrust Act, which stated that "labor is not a commodity." In effect, the new law declared that workers were people and should not be treated as if they were corporations. Unions were no longer subject to the punishing rules of the Sherman Antitrust Act. They could now legally strike, picket, and boycott employers.

In addition, the eight-hour workday became law nationally. Immigration was restricted, and a literacy test was imposed on immigrants. Although Congress passed a law forbidding child labor in industries involved in interstate commerce, the Supreme Court later struck it down. Finally, Sam no longer had to worry about going to jail for his contempt of court conviction. On May 11, 1914, the United States Supreme

Court overturned his conviction and those of his two colleagues.

Under Sam's leadership, the AFL emerged as the most important union in the country, powerful and respected. Elected officials sought out Sam for advice and support. Despite these successes, newspaper headlines emphasizing labor violence during strikes continued to portray unions in a bad light. Sam encouraged union members to avoid physical strife, telling one union, "When I say fight, I mean with your brains and your tongues, and not with bludgeons and pistols."

Over time, as the negative headlines faded from memory, Sam turned his attention to enhancing unions' image. A new headquarters building in Washington would show the world just how far the AFL had come from its tiny, ramshackle shed in New York. At noon on January 8, 1916, Sam proudly presided over the laying of the new building's cornerstone. He told the assembled group, "This structure of labor typifies all that is good and noble, and shall stand as an enduring monument which shall inspire the members of organized labor to carry the work through all times." Sam's son Henry, the AFL's first office boy and now a member of the Granite Cutters'

President Woodrow Wilson stands next to Sam as a parade passes by during the 1916 dedication ceremony for the new AFL Building in Washington, DC.

International Union, donated the stone and also engraved its inscription:

American Federation of Labor
Founded 1881
This edifice erected for service
In the cause of
Labor-Justice-Freedom-Humanity
1915–1916

Sam placed a sealed copper box containing letters from President Woodrow Wilson and other dignitaries inside the cornerstone. With immense pride, he also included autographed photographs of himself and four generations of Gompers family union members. Another son, Samuel, was a union printer, and a granddaughter, Florence, was a union stenographer. The oldest Gompers union member was Sam's father, eighty-nine-year-old Solomon.

A few months later, on July 4, 1916, over 10,000 enthusiastic union members gathered at the corner of Ninth Street and Massachusetts Avenue NW in Washington. They stood before the imposing new seven-story AFL headquarters as President Wilson dedicated the building. Under Sam's leadership, unions had come a long way in the previous thirty-five years. The membership of the AFL itself had grown from 200,000 to 3 million. Now American union members could point with pride to a permanent home among the historic monuments and buildings of the nation's capital.

Samuel Gompers and his closest advisors. Standing left to right: Max Morris, John B. Lennon, and John Mitchell. Seated left to right: James Duncan, Sam, and Frank Morrison.

SEVEN
LABOR GOES TO WAR

"War to suppress crime is justifiable; . . . I will induce my boys . . . to follow me."

—Samuel Gompers

All of his life, Sam had spoken out against war. This changed with the outbreak of World War I in 1914. Americans nervously followed events unfolding in Europe as the Allies (France, Great Britain, and Russia) fought the Central Powers (Germany and the Austro-Hungarian Empire). President Woodrow Wilson publicly insisted on American neutrality and urged citizens not to take sides in the war.

This was the world's first modern war, featuring the use of airplanes and tanks, as well as trench warfare. Sam viewed with horror Germany's introduction of poison gas and the targeting of civilian ships at sea. He told a union convention that this was the "most brutal and unholy war in the history of mankind." He publicly reversed his long-standing antiwar stance and later wrote, "I was no longer a pacifist." Anti-German feelings in the United States grew in 1915 after a German submarine sank the

Lusitania, an unarmed British passenger ship, resulting in the deaths of over 120 American passengers. Despite the public outcry, German submarines continued to attack unarmed ships.

Although Wilson's campaign slogan in the 1916 election was "He kept us out of war," he recognized that the United States could not remain neutral much longer. Shortly after the election, Wilson began preparing the country for war. Sam agreed with the president and later declared, "It was not possible for any important world-power to remain neutral." Like Wilson, he understood that sooner or later, the United States would enter the war against Germany.

In August 1916, Wilson created the Council of National Defense to coordinate government agencies preparing for war. He also created a seven-member Advisory Commission to the Council of National Defense to represent different segments of American society. Among the appointees were Julius Rosenwald, the president of Sears, Roebuck; Bernard Baruch, a financier; and Sam, who was named chairman of the Committee on Labor. The committee, which was made up of union leaders, employers, and bankers, pledged to keep American factories working without the threat of union disruptions. Sam was transformed from union spokesman to international diplomat.

As American entry into the war drew closer, a serious problem emerged on the United States' border with Mexico. As a result of the ongoing revolution in Mexico, armed bandits often crossed the border and attacked Americans. In 1916, the United States Army entered Mexico to stop the attacks. In the fighting that followed, several American soldiers were killed and others taken prisoner. As the prospect of war loomed over the two countries, Sam urged President Wilson not to retaliate. Especially given the possible entry of America into the world war, it was important to keep Mexico friendly toward the United States. Sam had a special relationship with Mexican labor and political leaders. Writing to Mexican president Venustiano Carranza, Sam called for peace and persuaded the president to release the American prisoners. He could rightly claim some credit for helping to prevent a war between the United States and Mexico.

On April 2, 1917, Wilson asked Congress to declare war against Germany. "The present German submarine warfare against commerce is a warfare against mankind," he proclaimed, and "a war against all nations." The United States should enter the war, he believed, because "the world must be made safe for democracy." In a recorded message, Sam explained labor's importance in the war effort: "This war is a people's war—labor's war. The final outcome will be determined in the factories, the mills, the shops, the mines, the farms, the industries." He later wrote, "The workers have a part in this war equal

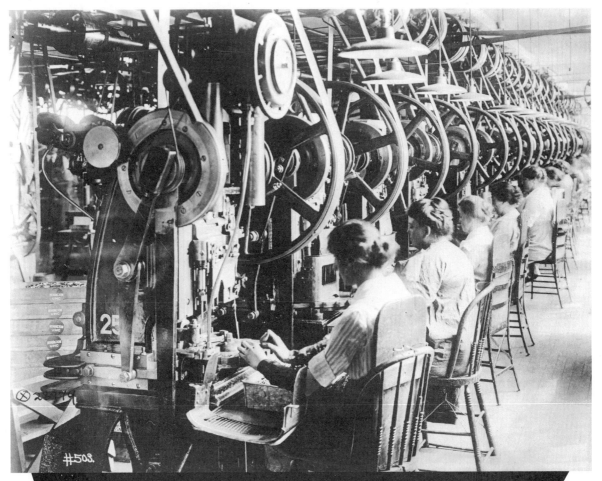
Women assemble cartridges in the Remington Arms Factory in Bridgeport, Connecticut, during World War I. As men went to war, women entered the workforce in large numbers.

with the soldiers and sailors." Without the coal, steel, munitions, tanks, and airplanes produced by American workers, there could be no victory.

The president was grateful for Sam's early and continuing support. On November 12, 1917, Wilson traveled to Buffalo, New York, to become the first American president to speak at the annual convention of the American Federation of Labor. During his address, Wilson said of Sam,

"I want to express my admiration of his patriotic courage, his large vision, and his statesmanlike sense of what has to be done."

Sam's support for the war effort was sincere. He was a patriotic American. Even during his antiwar years, he said, "I believe that we in the United States have the best country on the face of God's green earth." He worked closely with wartime officials to ensure that there would be no labor disruptions of the war effort. As the government began a massive construction project to build military bases across the country, everyone understood that in wartime, any delays could hurt the country's military. Sam and Secretary of War Newton D. Baker signed an agreement that set wartime labor standards for the construction industry, recognizing union contract wages, union-approved working conditions, and, most important to Sam, the eight-hour workday.

Employers who usually fought such standards accepted the new rules so that their businesses would not face work interruptions. Workers, no longer having to fight for their rights, were more than content with their union wages, benefits, and job security. Also included in the agreement were rules to peacefully resolve disputes. The construction agreement was successful and soon expanded to other vital industries.

Sam traveled around the country speaking about labor's support of the war effort. To great applause, he told one audience, "I count myself transformed from an ultra pacifist to a living, breathing, fighting man." He believed that "peace is impossible so long as life and liberty are challenged and menaced," and he looked upon the war as a turning point for workers' rights. Unions were now represented on national councils and received public recognition for their patriotic attitudes. Unemployment dropped from 7.9 percent

to 1.4 percent, and thanks to wartime labor regulations, workers' pay and benefits increased.

Across the country, as union membership increased, Labor Day celebrations in 1918 highlighted workers' contributions to the war effort. Sam optimistically believed that when the war ended, the positive feelings toward labor would continue. He confidently told one group, "Do you think those representatives of labor are to be thrown aside? Not on your life!"

In August 1918, at the request of President Wilson, Sam boarded a troop transport, the SS *Missanabie*, for a dangerous eleven-day voyage to Liverpool, England. He sailed with other union officials, including his longtime adviser, James Duncan, as chairman of the American Labor Mission to Europe. Their task was to show American support for European workers during wartime and to participate in European labor conferences. The group faced a harrowing voyage across the North Atlantic, where German submarines lurked.

Upon his safe arrival, one of Sam's first stops was in London and the Spitalfields neighborhood of his childhood. The houses hadn't changed much over the years, but Sam was now a celebrity. He visited the school in Bell Lane that he had attended for four years and addressed the students. As he had on previous visits to the city, he found time to reunite with relatives, many of whom he had never met before. At a

Like her husband, Sophia Gompers was not shy about making her views known. Here, she leads a demonstration urging citizens to conserve the use of sugar during World War I. She is shown (center) with noted author Mary Antin (left) and New York City's Deputy Market Commissioner, Mrs. Louis Reed Welzmiller (right).

gathering of about forty family members, he was particularly excited to reconnect with Clara Gompers Le Bosse, his father's sister. As delightful as the family reunion was, the highlight of his trip to England was a meeting with King George V and Queen Mary in Buckingham Palace. For Sam, born in London in humble circumstances, this was the greatest of honors.

He stopped by military hospitals to visit wounded American soldiers before heading off to the first labor conference of the trip, in Derby. Sam was the center of attention. One newspaper said, with some exaggeration, "No man in the United States, except the President himself, wields such power as does Mr. Gompers."

A week later, Sam returned to London to participate in yet another conference. There he struck out forcefully against the socialist and pacifist delegates who were seeking to hold meetings with German labor leaders even as the war continued. "Socialism holds nothing but unhappiness for the human race," he declared, ". . . and it has no place in the hearts of those who would secure and fight for freedom and preserve democracy."

From London, he was off to France. Among those greeting the delegation in Paris were Sam's French cousins Louis and Florence Gompers. Sam told his welcomers he was in their country to show American labor's continued support of France even as the fighting continued there. Along with giving speeches to labor groups, he saw firsthand the ravages of war. He offered comfort to the wounded in a military hospital and paid his respects to the dead in a temporary cemetery.

On roads packed with troops and trucks, he made his way to the front, where he struck up conversations with everyone from privates to generals. While picnicking with the British general Sir Douglas Haig in the fields between Arras and Cambrai, shells screamed over their heads and dropped around them. They sat on the ground and ate under the only remaining tree in sight, surrounded by dead soldiers and horses.

Next, he was off to Rome, where he met with government officials and local labor groups. In Padua, he dined with King Victor Emmanuel III. As in France, he headed off to the front, where American soldiers were stationed. The trip ended unexpectedly when Sam received sad news. His beloved and last surviving daughter, Sadie, had died of the Spanish flu on October 14. She was one of many casualties of the influenza, or flu, pandemic of 1918–1919, the deadliest in modern history. At a time before antibiotics, more than 25 percent of the United States population became sick, and some 675,000 Americans died.

Sam hurried back to Paris. Waiting for him at the hotel were seven letters from Sadie. He was overcome with grief as he read them. The two were very close, and he often relied on her for advice. Sadie, like Sam, enjoyed music. She was a trained singer and, with her father's encouragement, had embarked on a brief show business career, appearing nationally on the vaudeville stage. The sudden shock of her death, together with the rigor of his trip, led to a physical and emotional collapse. The cousins who had met Sam upon his earlier arrival in Paris summoned a physician and stayed by his bedside for two days until he improved and could obtain passage on the next ship bound for the United States.

Sam boarded the USS *Tenadores* in a state of depression. The ship was carrying wounded soldiers home, and despite his condition, he volunteered to spend time talking with and reading to them. He also did not hold back when passengers "insisted upon my addressing them." Never one to ignore an opportunity to speak, he later recalled, "I could not fail them."

The ship docked in Hampton Roads, Virginia. Sam took a train directly to New

Sadie Gompers was a talented singer who for a while performed publicly in vaudeville theaters. She was a strong supporter of her father and often accompanied him on union business trips.

York City, where Sadie would be buried in Washington Cemetery near other Gompers relations. Though gripped by sadness, Sam could not ignore his union responsibilities. Before the funeral on November 5, he issued a statement to the press reporting on his European trip and calling for continued support of President Wilson in the war effort. A few days later, on November 11, 1918, World War I ended.

Immediately after the funeral, Sam traveled to Chicago, where he told labor leaders that his mission abroad had "stiffened the spine of labor in allied countries." Then he was off to Laredo, Texas, to help organize the Pan-American Federation of Labor. With the support of President Wilson, Sam wanted to bring American trade union ideals to neighboring countries threatened by communist and socialist takeovers. The goal was to establish better understanding among the working people of the Americas. At the meeting were union members from Mexico, Chile, Cuba, Guatemala, Argentina, and Costa Rica, along with delegates from the AFL representing the United States. Those attending the meeting elected Sam president.

Within months, the good feelings about unions that had contributed so much to the American war effort began to disintegrate. Although Secretary of the Navy Josephus Daniels reported to President Wilson on the unions' wartime cooperation, saying that "much of this satisfactory condition is due to the loyal cooperation of the heads of the American Federation of Labor, with whom the department has maintained the friendliest relations," the president chose to pay more attention to employers who wanted to return to prewar conditions. With the fighting over, the government withdrew or ignored the wartime rules that had benefited workers. Many good jobs disappeared, and wages declined. Sam was disappointed with President Wilson's unexpected turn against labor.

By the end of the war, the AFL had grown to over 3.3 million members. At the thirty-ninth annual AFL convention in June 1919 in Atlantic City, New Jersey, Sam told the delegates, "Men and women shed their blood and made the great sacrifices during the war because they were fighting for principles and ideals. Now that the war has been won the workers—the bone and flesh of the nation—do not intend those principles and ideals shall be lost sight of."

Meanwhile, with all the support Sam had given Wilson in the war effort, he expected the president to appoint him as one of the American representatives to the Paris Peace Conference. Indeed, when British foreign secretary Lord Balfour was asked to name America's greatest contribution to the war, "he replied in one word: 'Gompers.'" But with the political climate now favoring business over labor, Wilson instead sent Sam and James Duncan to Paris to represent the United States on the International Labor Commission. Created by the Paris Peace Conference, the commission was charged with developing and overseeing rules on working conditions throughout the world. Sam boarded a ship for Europe on January 8, 1919. At the first meeting of the commission later that month, the members elected Sam as their chairman. Under his leadership, the commission created the International Labour Organization (ILO), which continues to exist today as an agency of the United Nations.

All the traveling, countless meetings,

and seemingly endless speechmaking took a toll on Sam. He was sixty-nine years old and suffered from high blood pressure, diabetes, kidney disease, and failing eyesight. He was in such poor health that, on March 31, he needed help walking up the gangplank of the *Rotterdam* for his return home. Ten days later, he felt better when the ship arrived in New York, where he was met by his sons Samuel and Alexander. They gently broke the news to him that his beloved wife, Sophia, had suffered a severe paralytic stroke. She had never recovered from the death of their daughter Sadie the previous fall. One friend observed that "the will to live had been crushed in her" by Sadie's death.

For years, Sophia, whom Sam called "Mother," had been the anchor in his life. Quiet and unassuming, she had avoided the public spotlight while supporting Sam completely through good times and bad. She had maintained a comfortable home, which had also served as an unofficial meeting place for AFL leaders. Everyone had been welcome. Although Sam was concerned about his wife's debilitated condition, there was little he could do for her, and so he concentrated on union business.

A surprise announcement by President Wilson boosted his morale. To show his appreciation for organized labor's cooperation before and during the war, Wilson proposed naming a cargo ship in honor of the American Federation of Labor.

It was a proud moment for Sam when he traveled to a shipyard in Philadelphia on June 28, 1919, for the launch ceremony. He himself had come up with the ship's name, *Afel*, based on the federation's initials. Sam was "moved by the spectacle of the huge ship" and delivered a short speech to the assembled workers in remembrance of the war effort. "At last the dawn of a new day has come," he said, "that for which you men labored in this greatest of shipyards."

Sam liked to be in charge, but even he could not control fate. In New York a few weeks later, the taxi in which he was riding was struck by a streetcar. The accident took place just outside his hotel, and bystanders carried him to his room, where doctors attended to him. He was badly injured, suffering two broken ribs. Sam revealed more bad news to a colleague who was visiting him. "I am going blind," he admitted. For the rest of his life, he was accompanied by someone at all times to help prevent him from falling. He never made his vision problem public. "Socialists have always called me blind," he once quipped. "What a field day they would have if they knew the truth!"

By July, he felt healthy enough to head back to Europe for a meeting of the International Federation of Trade Unions in Amsterdam. With the war over, the world's attention was now focused on Russia, where a communist revolution had overthrown the government in 1917. Sam, who had long believed that unions should be independent of revolutionary political movements, had a fight on his hands in Amsterdam. First, he gathered support to stop an attempt by German labor delegates who wanted to blame the world war on Britain and the United States. Next, he successfully led the opposition to a resolution endorsing the Russian Revolution.

Sam arrived home on August 26, returning to a changed America and the most dire labor situations of his career. With the war over, the country faced serious labor problems as workers in major industries protested worsening conditions. It was estimated that in 1919, nearly 20 percent of American workers went out on strike as courts overturned laws regarding picketing, child labor, and the minimum wage. Wartime patriotism gave way to the Red Scare, with people fearing a communist takeover by American radicals. (Communists and other radicals were often referred to as Reds because of the color of the Russian flag.) The successful Russian Revolution in 1917 created a concern that communism would spread to the United States. To add to the hysteria, a series of bombings by disgruntled anarchists further frightened Americans. Mistrust of foreigners grew, as many people attributed the growing number of strikes to communists and other radical groups. Two strikes especially received much public attention. The first was a national steel strike, and the second was a police strike in Boston. Both involved Sam directly.

In September 1919, 350,000 steelworkers, many of them immigrants, went on strike for higher wages and a forty-hour workweek. Although Sam publicly backed the strikers, he always argued against strikes that had no chance of succeeding and privately cautioned the steelworkers against striking. The public, fearing communist influence, reacted negatively to news reports of violent picketers. From the start of his union career, Sam had battled socialists and other radicals within the labor movement. Now the *New York Times* reported, "The authority and the leadership of Mr. Gompers are at stake in this strike. . . . He has no liking for the revolutionary element in labor."

Sam did his best to bring workers and employers together, but the president of United States Steel refused even to meet with him. President Wilson called for a national industrial conference, but his attempt failed as employers continued to refuse to engage in any meaningful discussions with workers. Sam defended the strikers before a United States Senate committee, telling senators, "The right to be heard is what the steel workers are asking above all else. . . . To have some voice in determining conditions under which they work."

When the strike ended in January 1920 without any concessions by employers, it was

State troopers prepare to deal with steel industry strikers, 1919. Labor unrest after World War I led to violence between striking workers and police.

disappointing to Sam. But another strike that year was more damaging to his reputation.

Also dissatisfied with working conditions, police officers in Boston formed a union on August 15, 1919. They applied to the AFL for membership and were granted a charter. This act angered the police commissioner, who fired the union leaders. In response, on September 9, the Boston police force went out on strike. The resulting rise in crime and looting led to headlines in newspapers across the country. Although it was far from the truth, many Americans blamed Sam and the AFL for the violence and believed that the strike was yet another communist plot.

Sam sympathized with the police officers but urged them to return to work because the public safety was in danger. He realized that the reputation of the

entire labor movement was at stake here. In a telegram sent on September 12, he appealed to the police union to return to work. When the officers finally understood that their strike was hopeless, they reluctantly agreed to resume their duties and begin arbitration. But now the city's police commissioner and Massachusetts governor Calvin Coolidge refused to rehire them. "There is no right to strike against the public safety," Coolidge declared, "by anybody, anywhere, any time." Coolidge's strong stand received national support. At least partly because of his firm actions, he was elected vice president of the United States in 1920 and became president upon the death of Warren Harding in 1923.

The strike was an embarrassment to the AFL, which was caught between its desire to help struggling police officers and the public fear of a communist plot. Not yet fully recovered from his accident in July, Sam suffered an attack of nervous exhaustion and fever in mid-October. His doctor ordered him to bed.

The following year, Sam traveled to Boston to address the Chamber of Commerce. The business leaders were not sympathetic to his explanation that the police officers' affiliation with the AFL was not a threatening or improper act. Even in front of that hostile audience, however, he did not back down. "I am not in the habit of running away from any issue," he said with a bit of humor. "Probably I have not been made on the running plan—my legs are too short."

Both personally and professionally, 1919 was "a most eventful year of sadness" for Sam. His father, Solomon, died on September 8 at the age of ninety-two. A friend was greatly impressed by the "love and reverence each of them had for one another." At a party shortly before Solomon's death, Sam had playfully put his hands over his father's eyes and asked him to guess who it was. After a few guesses, Solomon responded, "It is my boy, Sammy!" The "boy" was then nearly seventy years old and going blind like his father, who had been sightless for the past twenty years.

Sam refused to talk publicly about his own physical problems. On his seventieth birthday, on January 27, 1920, he told a reporter that "he felt as if he were only 40." He took the opportunity to admit, "My life has been most irregular. I cannot remember a time when I had to have my meals at a certain hour or set aside an hour to sleep. I ate when I could and slept when I could. The only influence that governed my meals and sleeping was my work."

Later that year, on May 6, after fifty-one years of marriage, Sam's wife, Sophia, died. Although her death was not unexpected, it was a major blow for Sam. Now nearly blind, in declining health, and feeling lonely without Sophia, Sam focused even more on his union work.

EIGHT
FIGHTER FOR FREEDOM

"I want to live for one thing alone—to leave a better labor movement in America and in the world than I found when I entered, as a boy."

—Samuel Gompers

Within a year of Sophia's death, Sam remarried. His new wife, Gertrude Neuscheler, was a divorcée he had met years earlier on a visit to Trenton, New Jersey, when she was still a teenager. Over the years, he had often been a guest in her parents' home. A few months after Sophia's death, Sam reunited with her. On their wedding day, Sam said he was "too happy for words." The joy did not last long.

Gertrude, a music teacher, was thirty years younger than Sam, but it was not age alone that separated them. Gertrude did not support his work, and many thought the only reason she married Sam was because he was famous. They argued constantly, and Gertrude even tried to control Sam's life by restricting his visitors. Given this difficult situation at home, he spent even more time at work, with no end of conferences, speaking, writing, and traveling. He confided to a friend, "I could not stop working if I wanted to."

Samuel Gompers and his second wife, Gertrude Neuscheler

Sam faced a growing number of challenges. The country slipped into an economic depression, resulting in increased unemployment. This led to a growing number of strikes and work disputes. Despite the Clayton Antitrust Act, courts granted more injunctions against union strikers.

Even with these mounting labor issues, Sam was in the forefront of major social changes sweeping America. He had strong opinions and, like his family members, was not shy about expressing them. When a reporter once asked his daughter, Sadie, if she was a suffragist—a supporter of women's right to vote—she quickly responded, "Yes, indeed," then added, "Mother and I are both strong believers in suffrage." Sophia Gompers, sounding like a union organizer, said that allowing women to vote would lead to "higher wages for women, shorter hours, better conditions, more unionism among women workers."

Sadie was proud of supporting women's rights "like dad."

In fact, Sam led organized labor to support the women's suffrage movement. He told union members, "There are two tremendous movements for freedom at the present time—the labor movement and the woman suffrage movement." He fought vigorously for the passage of the Nineteenth Amendment to the United States Constitution, which would give women the right to vote. "As a matter of justice," he wrote, "workingwomen demand the ballot." The amendment was adopted after a long fight on August 26, 1920.

With a growing and diverse AFL membership, Sam knew it was time to correct a wrong. Although the AFL's constitution officially supported equal

These young picketers' fathers were striking waiters at the Raleigh Hotel in Washington, DC, in 1919.

rights for African Americans, the federation continued to ignore discrimination by individual unions. Sam led the fight at the 1919 AFL convention that resulted not only in the federation granting membership equality to African Americans but also in the organization threatening to expel any union that discriminated against blacks. "It is one of the most important steps taken by the Federation in many years," Sam said.

But he was not as supportive of other groups. With growing fear of communists, socialists, anarchists, and foreigners in general, Congress began debating restricting the number of immigrants allowed into the United States. Sam backed a strict immigration quota system, which eventually became law with the passage of the Immigration Act of 1924. The act dramatically limited the number of people from eastern and southern Europe entering the country. Similarly, from his early days as a cigar union officer, he had championed the Chinese Exclusion Act of 1882 and the extension of that act in 1902. "We make no pretense," he wrote, "that the exclusion of Chinese can be defended upon a high ideal, ethical ground, but we insist that it is our essential duty to maintain and preserve our physical condition and standard of life and civilization."

At the same time, he continued to support the establishment of democratic labor organizations in other countries, particularly in nearby Latin America. Using his Freemasonry contacts, Sam advanced the cause of labor unions there. "In my Masonic life," he said, "I have visited lodges in many lands, and I have learned that Freemasonry in many

A large group of suffragists gather in 1916 to protest President Woodrow Wilson's opposition to women's right to vote. The women are carrying signs with slogans such as "Wilson Is Against Women" and "Vote Against Wilson He Opposes National Woman Suffrage."

countries, particularly in Latin countries, is the principal means whereby freedom of conscience, of thought, and expression is preserved."

Despite worsening health and vision problems, Sam traveled to Mexico City in 1921 to preside over the Pan-American Federation of Labor convention. Anti-American feelings were running high. The United States was involved militarily and politically in several Central American and Caribbean countries. With political instability in the region, the United States was concerned about the security of the Panama Canal. Opened in 1914, the Canal was a vital shipping route linking the Atlantic and Pacific oceans. Two years later, the United States Army had begun an eight-year occupation of the Dominican Republic

in order to control a chaotic and unstable political situation there. When delegates to the convention introduced a resolution condemning American occupation of that country, Sam fought against its passage. He succeeded in substituting a milder statement that only requested the United States government to hasten the evacuation of its troops. Throughout the meeting, socialists and communists tried to control events, but Sam prevailed and was reelected president of the federation by a nearly unanimous vote.

Back home, Sam faced growing opposition within his own ranks from those who thought he was becoming too cautious. Some members felt that he prevented the AFL from fighting for such popular demands as government unemployment

Samuel Gompers fought against the use of child labor. These child laborers left school to work in a factory. Now they are on strike, waiting to return to work once the strike is settled.

insurance and old-age pensions for workers. It was not that Sam opposed these ideas, but he wanted workers to obtain these benefits through collective bargaining with employers rather than through government actions. At the 1921 AFL convention, John L. Lewis, head of the United Mine Workers of America, opposed Sam for the presidency, but the delegates reelected Sam by a majority of nearly two to one.

In 1922, Sam renewed the fight to abolish child labor nationally. "The fight is still on," he said, "and will continue until this unhuman practice is stopped." Although individual states had adopted various child labor laws over the years, the results were not uniform. Sam accepted the position of permanent chairman of the National Child Labor Committee to advocate for a constitutional amendment to abolish child labor. After passing both houses of Congress in 1926, the Child Labor Amendment had to be ratified by at least three-quarters of the states in order to become part of the United States Constitution. Voters who felt that the amendment took away parents' rights to make decisions about their own children's lives raised enough opposition to prevent ratification. The amendment has never expired and could still be voted into law today.

A few years earlier, a different amendment entirely, which Sam opposed, had been passed by the states easily. For Sam, who had always enjoyed a good meal and a good beer, ratification of the Eighteenth Amendment on January 16, 1919, was a personal affront. He continued to oppose the result of that amendment, Prohibition, which banned the manufacture and sale of alcoholic beverages. "I know," he confessed, "what a glass of beer meant to me in the midday, in the factory full of

Government agents destroy barrels of beer with an ax, along the Schuylkill River in Pennsylvania, in 1924.

Sam believed that making alcohol illegal especially hurt workers. As someone who regularly enjoyed a beer or two, he opposed Prohibition. Here, he leads an anti-Prohibition demonstration in Washington, DC, in 1919.

dust, full of foul air." He further explained, "I worked in a factory for twenty-six years with my shop mates and I know what I am talking about. The lunch that a laboring man takes with him to his work by noon becomes nearly dried out. By chipping in with several others, he can procure a small amount of beer with which to wash it down and make it palatable. . . . And in the evening, perhaps a pitcher of beer with his supper. . . . It is not a question of right or wrong. It is not a question of whether we approve or disapprove of beer drinking. It is his habit." When a Prohibition supporter said that alcoholic drinks were the curse of the workingman, Sam corrected him: "It is the misery of poverty and overwork and undernourishment which has driven men to drink."

Sam celebrated his seventy-fourth birthday alone on January 27, 1924, by working all day. He and Gertrude now largely lived apart. She was more interested in pursuing a social life, and Sam was unwilling to devote less time to his union affairs. His health visibly declined, but he continued to maintain a grueling schedule of meetings, speeches, and office work. His frail body was failing, but his mind was as sharp as ever. He said that in the previous four months, he had "travelled more than 16,000 miles, delivered 210 addresses, presided at 300 conferences, and written thousands of letters and statements." He told the reporter, "I can't keep still, if I wanted to."

In May, he was hospitalized in New York for six weeks, as diabetes worsened his

Samuel Gompers is shown testifying before Congress on April 21, 1924. Sam understood that a key way to improve workers' lives was through legislation. Although he opposed AFL involvement with political parties, he supported pro-labor candidates. He also frequently appeared before Congress to testify about proposed laws that would benefit workers.

kidney and heart conditions. He had always liked to eat, but now doctors severely limited his diet. He could barely walk, but that did not stop him. With a doctor and nurse by his side, he presided over a union conference to prepare for the upcoming Democratic National Convention.

The AFL convention in 1924 was in El Paso, Texas. Sadly, everyone, including Sam, realized that this would be his last time presiding over the union he had founded and so loved. Plans called for Sam to travel to Mexico City after the convention to preside over the fourth congress of the Pan-American Federation of Labor, which he had also helped found. Mexico's newly elected president, Plutarco Elías Calles, a champion of workers' rights, had invited

Sam to participate in the presidential inauguration ceremonies scheduled to take place at the same time. "The president of the American Federation of Labor has a very distinct place in the hearts of the workers of Mexico," said Calles, who was a great admirer of Sam and the AFL.

Sam set out by train from Washington on November 9. He was accompanied by his eldest son, Samuel; his granddaughter Florence; a young great-granddaughter; AFL officials; and a nurse. The AFL convention was unlike previous ones, which had often been filled with noisy and sometimes angry debate. On the first day, after the delegates quickly concluded their official business, a sense of calm descended on the hall. Everyone there wanted to pay tribute to Sam.

His great-granddaughter led the nearly blind leader to his place on the platform. Too weak to deliver his opening speech himself, he handed it to William Green, an AFL vice president, to read. As Sam sat white-faced and shrunken in his seat of honor, he heard Green read his own words back to him: "Events of recent months have made me keenly aware that the time is not far distant when I must lay down my trust for others to carry forward." A reporter noted, "That sent a tremor through the convention hall that put it into a mood for further obeisance and homage. . . . What followed was even more stirring."

Coincidentally, the Mexican Federation of Labor was holding its convention just across the border in Juárez, Mexico. The afternoon at the AFL convention was much more festive than the morning, as delegates from the Mexican group crossed the border on foot and entered the convention hall to a rousing reception. They came to demonstrate their respect for Sam, who had worked so hard to improve working conditions in their country. The next day, the kindness was repaid as the American delegates crossed into Juárez to an equally cheerful reception by Mexican union members.

"This was not a convention, but a drama," the reporter wrote. The highlight occurred on the convention's sixth day. Morris Sigman of the International Ladies' Garment Workers' Union asked to speak before the delegates. As he paid an emotional tribute to Sam for his past support, a curtain parted behind Sam to reveal a carved bust of the ailing union leader. The audience gasped, rose to its feet, and applauded. Unable at first to understand what was happening, Sam turned slowly to discover the bust. He sank back into his chair as tears rolled down his face. He quickly regained control and said, "Nothing in the world so glorifies the soul as service to one's fellow-men," which led to more tears and sobs from the audience. Tough union workers "shed tears—bashfully, shamefacedly, but genuine tears."

Naturally, Sam was reelected president of the American Federation of Labor for the thirty-seventh year, this time unanimously. He banged down the gavel to close the convention with these words: "It is better to have resisted and failed than not to have resisted at all."

After the convention, Sam and three hundred delegates boarded a train for the three-day trip to Mexico City. There they entered a large stadium crowded with 50,000 Mexican union workers, who cheered Sam as he haltingly made his way up the stairs to the stage, supported on either side by friends. The warm welcome lifted his spirits. Sam and the newly elected president of the Mexican Federation of Labor embraced. Sam then left to open a meeting of the Pan-American Federation of Labor.

Against the advice of doctors, he attended several social events surrounding the inauguration of President Calles. The travel, public appearances, and high altitude of Mexico City affected the ailing labor leader's health. By December 7, he decided that he could not continue and returned to the United States. President Calles arranged for a special train for Sam, who was carried aboard on a stretcher. Calles and other government officials came to the train to bid Sam farewell. Sam told them, "I wish to live until I arrive in my own country; if I die I prefer to die at home."

Sam arrived in San Antonio, Texas, near death on December 13. He was taken to a hotel, where his closest colleagues kept watch as physicians and nurses attended to him. As Sam's last moments drew near, union officials who had supported him for years and whom he considered his extended family surrounded his bed. They included Frank Morrison, James Duncan, and Florence Thorne. Thorne's long association with the AFL had begun in 1910 when Sam hired her to work on the *American Federationist* and to research legislative and political issues.

Before Sam lost consciousness, Duncan, a Freemason, grasped his hand in the secret Masonic handshake, which Sam feebly acknowledged. Aware of his own place in history, he uttered these final words: "Nurse, this is the end. God bless our American institutions. May they grow better day by day." Eleven hours after returning to American soil, Samuel Gompers died.

News of his death spread quickly around the country. The funeral train carrying Sam's bronze, flag-draped casket began its slow journey east, first to Washington, DC, and finally to New York City, where funeral services would be held. Along the route, thousands of people gathered to mourn his death. At stops on the journey, local bands greeted the train with renditions of "Auld Lang Syne," and people filed onto the

train to pay their respects. In Washington, a military honor guard led his casket to a flower-filled room in the AFL building. An American flag and the bust presented to him in El Paso were displayed near the casket. Hundreds of mourners passed through the room. That evening, the casket was returned to the train for Sam's final trip to New York City.

The funeral service on December 17 was conducted in the large, ornate hall of the Elks Lodge. Sam's wife, children, and grandchildren were joined by hundreds of mourners, including the governor of New York and the mayor of New York City. The service was led by Rabbi Stephen S. Wise and broadcast live on radio. "Serving most the cause of organized labor," the rabbi said of Sam, "he best served America." As the funeral took place, the United States Senate interrupted its regular business so members could pay tribute to him.

As the funeral procession wound its way through the city, thousands lined the streets to bid him farewell. Police estimated that nearly 15,000 people were gathered in Times Square alone.

Sam was buried with a Masonic funeral service in Sleepy Hollow Cemetery in Sleepy Hollow, New York, about twenty-five miles north of New York City. As the casket was lowered into the ground, his friend and union colleague James Duncan delivered a message that Sam had given him just days earlier: "Say to the organized workers of America that as I have kept the faith I expect that they will keep the faith. They must carry on."

Although the fight to improve the lives of American workers would continue after his death, Sam once told a reporter, his life's work had been "to make to-morrow a better day for the laboring class."

Samuel Gompers' death left a profound void in the American labor movement. A San Francisco ironworker pauses on top of a forty-story building in tribute to Sam at the very hour that his funeral was taking place in New York in 1924.

EPILOGUE

"My work was my life."

—Samuel Gompers

Before the American Federation of Labor was founded, the typical American worker toiled six days a week, often more than fourteen hours a day. Workers could lose their jobs for no reason. Working conditions were unhealthy and unsafe. Unions were small, local, and mostly powerless. Samuel Gompers created a national organization that became a powerful force in the country's political and industrial life. The AFL helped bring about improvements in workers' lives that we take for granted today.

In 1907, an exposition in Jamestown, Virginia, commemorated the three hundredth anniversary of the first permanent English settlement in America.

One exhibit hall was designed by the AFL to highlight the skills and diversity of union members. Many products of organized labor were represented, including the handiwork of the "shoemaker, sawmaker, saddlemaker, harnessmaker, horseshoer, slatemaker, shinglemaker, glovemaker, furrier, cutler, baker, upholsterer, pianomaker . . . all bearing the labels of their respective crafts." In a place of honor over the entrance was a large picture of Sam. Today, more than one hundred years later, many of these occupations have vanished, but workers continue to enjoy the benefits Sam fought so hard for.

Thanks to Sam, American workers in the twenty-first century have these basic rights:

An eight-hour workday

A five-day workweek

Workers' compensation for injuries

A safe and healthy work environment

Due process for removal from a job

Minimum wage requirements

Strict child labor laws

At a time when some workers embraced radical or socialist agendas, Sam insisted on working within the American capitalist system. Throughout his union life, Sam expressed pride in the United States and strongly supported American values and traditions. He deeply believed that "America is not merely a name, a land, a country, a continent; America is a symbol. It is an ideal, the hope of the world."

A union's responsibility, he said, was not to pursue revolution, but to focus strictly on "pure and simple" unionism: shorter hours, higher wages, and better working conditions. "It is our duty," he told union members, "to live our lives as workers in the society in which we live, and not to work for the downfall or the destruction, or the overthrow of that society." Sam's faith in America and its traditions protected the AFL from the radical groups that believed in revolution and that workers and bosses had nothing in common. Although he initially opposed the AFL's involvement in politics, he eventually encouraged union members to participate actively in the political system.

After Sam's death, the AFL began softening its focus on organizing only skilled workers rather than all workers in a specific trade. Beginning with the Great Depression in 1929, as factories closed and unemployment rose, union membership dropped. In 1935, a number of AFL unions, led by the United Mine Workers of America, formed the Committee for Industrial Organization. The next year, the AFL retaliated by suspending these unions, and two years later, in 1938, the committee held its first convention and renamed itself the Congress of Industrial Organizations (CIO). The CIO opened membership to all workers in mass-production industries, including auto, steel, textile, and electrical product factories. After two decades of competition, the AFL and CIO merged in 1955 to form the American Federation of Labor–Congress of Industrial Organizations (AFL-CIO), America's largest union.

The AFL was founded with 200,000 members. At the time of his death, Sam counted nearly 4 million members—men and women of every race, religion, and political persuasion. Twenty-five years later, in 1949, AFL membership exceeded 10 million. In 1983, there were 17 million members, slightly more than 20 percent of all American workers. After that, union membership began to decline rapidly as large numbers of American factories closed and jobs moved overseas. With the upheaval in American manufacturing, it is no surprise that by 2017 the percentage of union members dropped to under 11 percent of American workers. Over 35 percent of Americans in public-sector positions (teachers, police officers, firefighters, etc.) were union members. Only 6.4 percent of private-sector workers were union members.

Whether someone today is a union member or not, all American workers continue to benefit from Sam's tireless efforts. Although he has been dead for more than ninety years, he is memorialized by school buildings, statues, and postage stamps. He is still honored as the great champion of workers not only in the United States but also around the world. Though short of stature, he projected the image of a giant. "I never got tired and gave any thought to my body," he once said, "for it never demanded my attention. The Gomperses are built of oak."

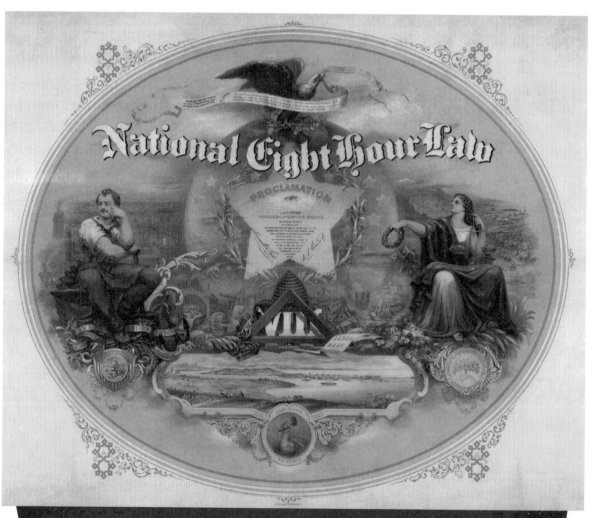

A poster marking President Ulysses S. Grant's 1869 signing into law of an eight-hour workday for government employees. Samuel Gompers fought throughout his life for a national eight-hour workday. He believed this was the first step to improve working conditions.

AUTHOR'S NOTE

Although I was born decades after Samuel Gompers's death, I feel as if I grew up with him. My father was the longtime secretary-treasurer and business agent of AFL Local 22114, the Wool Sorters' Union. I was probably the only sixth grader to regularly read the *American Federationist*, the official AFL magazine founded by Gompers. The names of Gompers, Green, George Meany, and other union leaders were as familiar to me as more famous historical figures. I remember accompanying my father to the local Labor Lyceum for union meetings. An ingrained family practice was never to cross a union picket line.

With that legacy, it has been a pleasure to research and tell Samuel Gompers's life story to a new generation of readers. I greatly appreciate the help of the following: Neera Puttapipat, IWM (Imperial War Museum) London; Jane Hodkinson, Manchester (England) Central Library; Kris Kinsey, University of Washington Libraries, Special Collections; Dov Smith, JFS School, Kenton, England; Harvey Sukenic, library director at Hebrew College; librarians and archivists at the UCLA (University of California, Los Angeles) Library and the USC (University of Southern California) Libraries. Special thanks go to Paul F. Cole, executive director of the American Labor Studies Center.

As always, I am grateful to two special people for making this book possible. First, to Carolyn Yoder, an editor's editor, who makes my writing coherent, and to my wife, Rosalind, for her patience and support.

—NHF

TIMELINE

1850	Samuel Gompers born January 27 in Spitalfields, London, England
1860	Leaves school to become shoemaker, then cigar maker
1863	Gompers family immigrates to United States
1864	Joins Cigar Makers' Union Local 15
1867	Marries Sophia Julian
1868	Sophia and Sam's first son, Samuel, born
1870	Son David born; dies in childhood before age ten
1870s	Economic depression results in large-scale unemployment
1872	Becomes United States citizen
	Daughter Rosetta (Rose) born
1874	Son Henry born
1875	Becomes first president of Cigar Makers' International Union of America Local 144
1876	Son Abraham born
1878	Son Alexander born
1882	First Labor Day Parade takes place, in New York City
	Chinese Exclusion Act
1883	Daughter Sadie born
1886	Haymarket riot in Chicago
	American Federation of Labor founded; Sam elected first president
1892	Homestead Strike
1894	Pullman Strike
1895	Serves as delegate to British Trades Union Congress
1898	Daughter Rose dies at age twenty-six
1900	Helps create National Civic Federation
1903	Son Abraham dies at age twenty-seven of tuberculosis
1905	Industrial Workers of the World (IWW) founded
1906	Presents "Labor's Bill of Grievances" to President Theodore Roosevelt and members of Congress

1908	Supreme Court ruling in Loewe & Company's case against hatters
	Buck's Stove and Range Company case against AFL; Sam and two other AFL officials found guilty of contempt of court following ruling against union
1909	Travels to Europe
	Court of appeals upholds Sam's and other two AFL leaders' contempt convictions
	Uprising of the 20,000
1910	Supports McNamara brothers, accused of bombing *Los Angeles Times* building
1911	Triangle Shirtwaist Factory fire
1913	United States Department of Labor created
1914	United States Supreme Court overturns Sam's and other two AFL leaders' contempt convictions
1917	United States enters World War I
	Named chair of a government advisory committee on labor
1918	Member of AFL delegation that travels to Europe; visits troops in France and Italy
	Daughter Sadie dies at age thirty-five of Spanish flu
	World War I ends
	Participates in conference of Pan-American Federation of Labor in Texas
1919	Returns to Europe to participate in International Labor Commission
	National steelworkers' strike begins
	Boston Police Strike
	Solomon Gompers dies at age ninety-two
1920	Wife Sophia dies at age seventy
1921	Marries Gertrude Neuscheler
1924	Presides over his last AFL convention
	Samuel Gompers dies December 13 at age seventy-four
1938	Son Henry dies at age sixty-four
1946	Son Samuel dies at age seventy-seven
1955	The AFL and the CIO merge

SOURCE NOTES

The source of each quotation in this book is found below. The citation indicates the first words of the quotation and its document source. The sources are listed either in the bibliography or below.

CHAPTER ONE

"A Prince in My Own Realm": Samuel Gompers (hereafter cited as Gompers), quoted in Stearn, p. 19.

"I loved the freedom . . .": Gompers, *Seventy Years*, v. 1, p. 45.

"endless rows of shabby houses . . .": Ibid., p. 16.

"sitting-room, bedroom, dining-room . . .": Ibid., p. 2.

"the great spiritual purpose . . .": Ibid., p. 17.

"To the West . . .": Cited ibid., p. 19.

"Any one of you . . .": Solomon Gompers, quoted ibid., p. 24.

"felt that some great power . . .": Gompers, quoted in Chasan, p. 23.

"for the privilege of looking . . .": Ibid.

"That is Mr. Gompers . . .": Stachelberg, quoted ibid., p. 64.

"A leaf of tobacco . . .": "Cigar Makers of London," Gen Pals, genpals.co.uk/cigars.php.

"I loved the touch . . .": Gompers, quoted in Weisberger, p. 18.

"I am an American . . .": Gompers, quoted in *Logansport* (Indiana) *Pharos-Tribune*, February 7, 1891.

"I never was an aspirant . . .": Gompers, *Seventy Years*, v. 1, p. 31.

"Study your union card . . .": Laurrell, quoted ibid., p. 75.

"the relations between . . .": Gompers, quoted in Weisberger, p. 136.

"life was becoming . . .": Ibid.

CHAPTER TWO

"No More Talk . . .": Quoted in Gompers, *Seventy Years*, v. 1, p. 54.

"Eight hours for work . . .": Ibid.

"He found what he called . . .": William Green, "Commemorating the Birth of the Champion of Human Well-Being," in *Golden Anniversary Commemorative Edition of Organized Labor* (San Francisco: Organized Labor Publishing, 1950), p. 21.

"We mean to uphold . . .": Quoted in Carroll Wright, "An Historical Sketch of the Knights of Labor," *Quarterly Journal of Economics* 1, no. 2 (1887): 143.

"It was an orgy . . .": Gompers, *Seventy Years*, v. 1, p. 96.

"The persons arrested . . .": *New York Times*, January 14, 1874.

"The cigars so made . . .": "The Cigar Makers' Strike," *New York Times*, September 2, 1877.

"You are not a very tall man . . .": Grant, quoted in Weisberger, p. 163.

"Yes, but I am not . . .": Gompers, quoted ibid.

"When we see . . .": Gompers to George Hurst, December 21, 1875, Samuel Gompers Papers Project. gompers.umd.edu.

"It provided him . . .": Livesay, p. 51.

CHAPTER THREE

"Full of Fire . . .": Gompers, *Seventy Years*, v. 1, p. 162.

"Never permit sentiment . . .": Laurrell, quoted ibid.

"When I enter . . .": Gompers, *Seventy Years*, v. 1, p. 458.

"there is not a dollar . . .": Gompers, quoted in Weisberger, p. 33.

"No local union . . .": Gompers, *Seventy Years*, v. 1, p. 169.

"Tenement-house Cigar-Making . . .": Quoted in *New York Times*, April 1, 1882, p. 5.

"Two Companions . . .": Ibid.

"a typical family . . .": "Tenement House Manifesto," *New Yorker Volkszeitung*, October 31, 1881, quoted in encyclopedia.com/history/encyclopedias-almanacs-transcripts-and-maps/gompers-samuel-2.

"Tobacco in every stage . . .": Gompers, quoted in Samuel Gompers Papers Project, v. 1, p. 174.

"Tobacco was everywhere . . .": Graffenried, quoted in Felt, p. 10.

"The manufacture of cigars . . .": Quoted in Fred Rogers Fairchild, "The Factory Legislation of the State of New York," *Publications of the American Economics Association* 6 (November 1905): 16.

"Well, what did you . . .": Gompers, *Seventy Years*, v. 1. p. 155.

"What do you suppose . . .": Sophia Gompers, quoted ibid.

"Good God, Sam . . .": Ibid., pp. 155–56.

"his distinctive idealism . . .": Weisberger, p. 32.

"I worked and supported . . .": Gompers, quoted in Gilson Gardner, "President of the American Federation of Labor Has No Money . . . ," *Pittsburg Press*, December 23, 1906, p. 3.

"We will fight for eight hours": Cited in Gompers, *Seventy Years*, v. 1, p. 54.

"a consolidated organization . . .": Quoted in Livesay, p. 84.

"simply did the best . . .": Gompers, *Seventy Years*, v. 1, p. 270.

"Many a time the children . . .": Ibid., p. 274.

"needed a central office . . .": Livesay, p. 85.

CHAPTER FOUR

"What Does Labor Want?": Gompers, quoted in "Samuel Gompers: Quotes," Goodreads, goodreads.com/quotes/109897.

"We want more . . .": Ibid.

"a stable membership . . .": Mandel, p. 210.

"learned the secret...": Gompers, quoted in *Princeton Union*, November 5, 1908.

"The best leaders . . .": Gompers, quoted ibid.

"The eight hour day . . .": *Rocky Mountain News*, April 23, 1890, p. 4.

"Our Federation was poor . . .": Gompers, *Seventy Years*, v. 1, p. 343.

"The stronger the union . . .": Ibid., p. 286.

"strengthen your position . . .": Gompers, quoted in Chasan, p. 59.

"If it takes the entire army . . .": Cleveland, quoted ibid., p. 76.

"Labor Day differs . . .": Gompers, quoted in Pennsylvania AFL-CIO, "Pennsylvania AFL-CIO: Labor Day Is Our Holiday," PR Newswire, August 30, 2011, prnewswire.com/news-releases/pennsylvania-afl-cio-labor-day-is-our-holiday-128697978.html.

"to voice the demands . . .": Gompers, "Salutatory," *American Federationist*, March 1894, p. 10.

"collective ownership . . .": Quoted in Harvey, p. 73.

"'I am entirely at variance . . .'": Gompers, quoted in Chasan, p. 73.

"After killing me . . .": Gompers, quoted in Mandel, p. 156.

"That trip constituted . . .": Gompers, *Seventy Years*, v. 1, p. 364.

"That southern trip . . .": Ibid., p. 365.

"For They Are Jolly...": Quoted in *Fort Wayne Weekly Gazette*, September 12, 1895.

"Samuel Gompers is one . . .": *Buffalo News*, quoted in "Conservative Triumph in the Federation of Labor," *Literary Digest*, December 28, 1895, p. 7.

CHAPTER FIVE

"Stand faithfully by our friends . . .": *Fort Wayne Sentinel,* July 22, 1908, p. 8.

"You shall not crucify . . .": "William Jennings Bryan Cross of Gold Speech July 8, 1896," American History from

Revolution to Reconstruction and Beyond, let.rug.nl/usa/documents/1876-1900/william-jennings-bryan-cross-of-gold-speech-july-8-1896.php.

"Some way must be found . . .": Gompers, quoted in Livesay, p. 94.

"I have no prejudice . . .": Gompers, *Seventy Years*, v. 2, p. 161.

"At best the profession . . .": "Address of Samuel Gompers," *Advocate of Peace*, April 1, 1897, p. 87.

"Upon the masses . . .": Ibid.

"It has been a splendid . . .": Hay, quoted in John H. Gable, "Credit 'Splendid Little War' to John Hay," letter to the editor, *New York Times*, July 9, 1991.

"glad of aid for the Cuban . . .": Gompers, *Seventy Years*, v. 2, p. 65.

"We cannot annex . . .": Gompers, quoted in Stephen Bender, "Recalling the Anti-Imperialist League," Antiwar. com, January 13, 2005, antiwar.com/orig/bender.php?articleid=4335.

"If the Philippines . . .": Gompers, "Imperialism—Its Dangers and Wrongs," speech, October 18, 1898, Freedom: A History of Us, tc.pbs.org/wnet/historyofus/web09/features/source/docs/C14.pdf.

"I tried to finish . . .": Gompers, Seventy Years, v. 1, pp. 422–23.

"He cannot speak . . .": "Mr. Gompers' Injuries," *Washington Evening Star*, December 7, 1899.

"There is only . . .": "Samuel Gompers Badly Hurt," *New York Times*, June 29, 1901.

"there is no occasion to fear . . .": "Mr. Gompers' Condition," *Washington Times*, June 29, 1901.

"Time and time again . . .": Gompers, quoted in Chasan, p. 106.

"Mr. Gompers, I want you to understand . . .": Roosevelt, quoted in Stearn, p. 93.

"Mr. President, I want you to understand . . .": Gompers, quoted ibid.

"I was convinced . . .": Gompers, quoted in Livesay, p. 138.

"At the present time . . .": Gompers, quoted in George Kibbe Turner, "What Organized Labor Wants, An Interview with Samuel Gompers." *McClure's Magazine*, November 1908, p. 30.

"A law that denies . . .": "Gompers, Mitchell and Morrison Get Jail Sentences; Give Bail Pending Appeal to U.S. Supreme Court," *Billings* (Montana) *Gazette*, December 25, 1908, p. 1.

"an invasion of the liberty . . .": "Gompers Defies Court," *New York Times*. January 25, 1908, p. 1.

"Let the slogan go forth . . .": Gompers to Millard Pettingill, April 25, 1906, in Gompers, *Gompers Papers*, v. 7, gompers.umd.edu/AFL%20Pettingill%201906.htm.

CHAPTER SIX

"Justice has been done . . .": Wilson, quoted in Livesay, p. 169.

"Laboring men and women . . .": Samuel Gompers, "Talks on Labor," *American Federationist*, May 1905, p. 371.

"the I.W.W. was frankly . . .": Gompers, *Seventy Years*, v. 1, p. 425.

"rainbow chasers": Gompers, quoted in "IWW," Samuel Gompers Papers, gompers.umd.edu/IWW.htm.

"found it necessary . . .": Gompers, quoted in James Creelman, "Mr. Gompers and His Two Million Men," *Pearson's Magazine*, September 1908, p. 250.

"Labor's Bill of Grievances": Stearn, p. 63.

"we shall appeal . . .": Quoted ibid., p. 65.

"I got hearings, sympathy . . .": Gompers, *Seventy Years*, v. 2, p. 257.

"We asked for bread . . .": Gompers, quoted in Chasan, p. 112.

"to get in closer touch . . .": Gompers, quoted in Eva McDonald Valesh, 'Au Revoir' to Samuel Gompers," *American Federationist*, July 1909, p. 607.

"I say, friends . . .": Gompers, quoted in Finkelstein, p. 22.

"to stand together . . .": Ibid.

"taking advantage of . . .": Gompers quoted in "Hostile Employers, See Yourselves As Others Know You." *American Federationist*, 1911, p. 356.

"people who created . . .": "Look for the Union Label," Massachusetts AFL-CIO, massaflcio.org/look-union-label.

"Every time you buy goods . . .": "Are You True to Yourself?," *American Federationist*, August 1919, p. 661.

"besmirch the name . . .": "Gompers Denounces Arrests as a Plot," *New York Times*, April 24, 1911.

"a painstaking, conscientious . . .": Gompers, quoted ibid.

"How long are the American people . . .": Gompers, quoted in "Labor Leaders Brand Dynamite Arrest as Plot," *Washington Times*, April 23, 1911, p. 1.

"The whole thing . . .": Gompers, quoted in "Asks Big Strike to Aid M'namara," *Chicago Tribune*, May 1, 1911, p. 1.

"It's all right . . .": McNamara, quoted in "Gompers and Burns on Unionism and Dynamite," *McClure's Magazine*, February 1912, p. 375.

"Sam, I want . . .": Ibid.

"I was horror struck . . .": Ibid, p. 375.

"The McNamaras have betrayed . . .": Gompers, quoted in "Gompers Is Amazed by the Confessions," *New York Times*, December 2, 1911.

"declaring their continued confidence . . .": Quoted in "Vote of Confidence in President Gompers," *Ladies' Garment Worker*, January 1912, p. 10.

"What was done . . .": Gompers, quoted in "Gompers Is Amazed."

"There are two tremendous . . .": Gompers, quoted in "Gompers Appeals for Suffragists," *New York Times*, September 15, 1915.

"labor is not a commodity . . .": Quoted in Livesay, p. 169.

"When I say fight . . .": Samuel Gompers, "Talks on Labor," *American Federationist*, December 1906, p. 91.

"This structure of labor . . .": Gompers, quoted in "Stone Laid for Labor Building," *Washington Herald*, January 9, 1916.

CHAPTER SEVEN

"War to suppress . . .": Gompers, quoted in Livesay, p. 176.

"most brutal and unholy . . .": Gompers, quoted in "Gompers Denounces War," *New York Times*, September 24, 1914.

"I was no longer a pacifist": Gompers, *Seventy Years*, v. 2, p. 331.

"He kept us out of war": Cited in "Woodrow Wilson," White House, whitehouse.gov/1600/presidents//woodrowwilson.

"It was not possible . . .": Gompers, *Seventy Years*, v. 2, p. 334.

"The present German submarine . . .": Wilson, quoted in Dantan Wernecke, "The World Must Be Made Safe for Democracy," TeachingAmericanHistory.org, April 1, 2012, teachingamericanhistory.org/past-programs/hfotw/120401-2/.

"the world must . . .": Ibid.

"This war is a people's war": Gompers, quoted in "Volume 10: Introduction," Samuel Gompers Papers, gompers.umd.edu/intro10.htm.

"The workers have a part...": loc.gov/item/today-in-history/april-06/

"I want to express . . .": Woodrow Wilson, "Labor Must Be Free," speech, November 12, 1917, American Presidency Project, presidency.ucsb.edu/ws/?pid=65402.

"I believe that we . . .": Gompers, "Talks on Labor," *American Federationist*, December 1906, p. 91.

"I count myself transformed . . .": "Address by Samuel Gompers," February 22, 1918, in *Labor's Attitude* (Washington, DC: Committee on Public Information, March 1918), p. 3.

"peace is impossible . . .": "Samuel Gompers on U.S. Conscription Policy, 1917," FirstWorldWar.com, firstworldwar.com/source/usconscription_gompers.htm.

"Do you think . . .": Gompers, quoted in "Gompers Pledges America's Labor to Nation in War," *New York Times*, February 23, 1918, p. 5.

"No man in the United States . . .": *New York Times*, quoted in Herbert W. Horwill, "British Labor and Mr. Gompers," *The Nation*, October 12, 1918, p. 415.

"Socialism holds nothing . . .": Gompers, quoted in Gompers, *Seventy Years*, v. 2, p. 431.

"insisted upon my addressing . . .": Gompers, *Seventy Years*, v. 2, p. 472.

"I could not fail . . .": Ibid.

"stiffened the spine . . .": Gompers, quoted in *New York Times*, November 9, 1918, p. 1.

"much of this . . .": Josephus Daniels, "Labor's Patriotic Part," *American Federationist*, January 1919, p. 51.

"he replied in one word . . .": Mandel, p. 416.

"the will to live . . .": Quoted in Chasan, p. 135.

"moved by the spectacle . . .": Matthew Woll, "The 'Afel.' American Labor's Ship, Launched With Fitting Ceremony," *American Federationist*, August 1919, p. 701.

"At last the dawn . . .": Gompers, quoted ibid.

"I am going blind": Gompers, quoted in Chasan, p. 136.

"Socialists have always . . .": Gompers, quoted in "Volume 11: Introduction," Samuel Gompers Papers, gompers.umd.edu/intro11.htm.

"The authority and the leadership . . .": *New York Times*, quoted in "The Steel Strike as a Labor Crisis," *Literary Digest*, October 11, 1919, p. 12.

"The right to be heard . . .": Gompers, quoted in "Recognition of Workers' Right to Organize Issue of Steel Strike, Gompers Tells Senate," *San Francisco Chronicle*, September 27, 1919.

"There is no right to strike . . .": Coolidge, p. 8.

"I am not in the habit . . .": Gompers, "Boston Police and the A.F. of L.," *American Federationist*, February 1920, p. 134.

"a most eventful year . . .": Gompers, quoted in "Volume 11: Introduction."

"love and reverence . . .": Daniel J. Tobin, "Remembrance of Sam Gompers," *International Teamster*, January 1950, v. 47, p. 10.

"It is my boy, Sammy!": Solomon Gompers, quoted ibid.

"he felt as if . . .": "Gompers Turned 70 Says He Feels 40," *New York Times*, January 28, 1920.

"My life has been most irregular . . .": Gompers, quoted ibid.

CHAPTER EIGHT

"I want to live for one thing . . .": Gompers, quoted in Irwin Yellowitz, "Samuel Gompers: A Half Century in Labor's Front Rank," *Monthly Labor Review*, July 1989, p. 27.

"too happy for words": Gompers, quoted in "Gompers Goes on Honeymoon with Bride to Toronto," *Washington Herald*, April 17, 1921.

"I could not stop working . . .": Gompers, quoted in "Volume 12: Introduction," Samuel Gompers Papers, gompers.umd.edu/intro12.htm.

"Yes, indeed": Sadie Gompers, quoted in "Miss Gompers a Suffragist," *Washington Herald*, December 16, 1913, p. 8.

"Mother and I . . .": Ibid.

"higher wages for women . . .": Sophia Gompers, quoted in "Miss Gompers a Suffragist," p. 8.

"like dad". . . "Daughter of President of A.F.L. Is Said to Be Engaged to George B. Gerau," *Washington Herald*, December 19, 1913.

"There are two tremendous . . .": Gompers, quoted in "Gompers Appeals for Suffragists," *New York Times*, September 15, 1915.

"As a matter of justice . . .": Gompers, quoted in International News Service, "Gompers in Favor of Woman Suffrage," *Los Angeles Herald*, September 15, 1915.

"It is one of the most important . . .": Gompers, quoted in "The Negro Enters the Labor-Union," *Literary Digest*, June 28, 1919, p. 12.

"We make no pretense . . .": Gompers, "American Labor and Immigration—Gompers Letter (Reprint)," special anniversary issue, *Social Contract* 15, no. 4 (Summer 2005): thesocialcontract.com/artman2/publish/tsc1504/article_1339.shtml

"In my Masonic life . . .": Gompers, quoted in Daniel, p. 460.

"The fight is still on . . .": Gompers, quoted in Robert G. Morris, "Gompers Will Renew Fight for Abolition of Child Labor," *Washington Times*, June 9, 1922, p. 3.

"I know what a glass of beer . . .": Gompers, quoted in Weisberger, p. 223.

"I worked in a factory . . .": Gompers, "Labor and Beer," *McClure's Magazine*, June 1919, p. 30.

"It is the misery . . .": Gompers, quoted in Mandel, p. 493.

"travelled more than 16,000 miles . . .": Associated Press, "Gompers Is 74, Forgot Sunday Was Birthday," *Shreveport Times*, January 28, 1924, p. 10.

"I can't keep still . . .": Gompers, quoted ibid.

"The president of the . . .": Calles, quoted in *Chicago Tribune*, August 9, 1924.

"Events of recent months . . .": Gompers, quoted in Frank Tannenbaum, "Samuel Gompers' Last Convention," *The Survey*, January 1, 1925, p. 391.

"That sent a tremor . . .": Tannenbaum, "Samuel Gompers' Last Convention," p. 391.

"This was not a convention . . .": Ibid., p. 394.

"Nothing in the world . . .": Gompers, quoted in "Labor to Stay Non-Partisan," *Shreveport Times*, November 25, 1924, p. 7.

"shed tears . . .": Tannenbaum, "Samuel Gompers' Last Convention," p. 394.

"It is better . . .": Gompers, quoted ibid.

"I wish to live . . .": Gompers, quoted in "Gompers Is Sinking as His Train Races Toward the Border," *New York Times*, December 12, 1924.

"Nurse, this is the end . . .": Gompers, quoted in "End Comes on Home Soil," *New York Times*, December 14, 1924.

"Serving most the cause . . .": Wise, quoted in "Thousands Pay Last Tribute to Gompers," *New York Times*, December 19, 1924.

"Say to the organized workers . . .": Duncan, quoted in Mandel, p. 530.

"to make to-morrow . . .": Gompers, quoted in Turner, "What Organized Labor Wants," p. 31.

EPILOGUE

"My work was my life": Gompers, quoted in Robert W. Bruere, "Gompers: The Source of His Power," *The Survey*, February 1, 1925, p. 541.

"shoemaker, sawmaker . . .": C. P. Connelly, "A.F. of L. Exhibit at Jamestown," *American Federationist*, August 1907, p. 563.

"America is not merely a name . . .": Gompers, "Our Shield Against Bolshevism," *McClure's Magazine*, April 1919, p. 10.

"pure and simple": Joseph C. Carter, "Samuel Gompers: Labor Pioneer, Crusader, and Statesman," *Mark Twain Journal* 10, no. 1 (Summer 1955): 20.

"It is our duty . . .": Gompers, quoted ibid., p. 16.

"I never got tired . . .": Gompers, quoted in Carter, "Samuel Gompers: Labor Pioneer," p. 18.

BIBLIOGRAPHY

BOOKS

Butterfield, Roger. *The American Past*. New York: Simon & Schuster, 1957.

Chasan, Will. *Samuel Gompers: Leader of American Labor*. New York: Praeger Publishers, 1971.

Coolidge, Calvin. *Law and Order*. Chicago: Donnelley, 1920.

Cooper, Patricia A. *Once a Cigar Maker*. Urbana: University of Illinois Press, 1992.

Daniel, John. *Two Faces of Freemasonry*. Longview, TX: Day Publishing, 2007.

Dubofsky, Melvyn, and Foster Rhea Dulles. *Labor in America: A History*. Somerset, NJ: Wiley, 2014.

Felt, Jeremy. *Hostages of Fortune: Child Labor Reform in New York State*. Syracuse, NY: Syracuse University Press, 1965.

Finkelstein, Norman H. *Forged in Freedom: Shaping the Jewish-American Experience*. Philadelphia: Jewish Publication Society, 2002.

Gompers, Samuel. *The Samuel Gompers Papers*. 12 vols. Urbana: University of Illinois Press, 1986–2010.

———. *Seventy Years of Life and Labor*. 2 vols. New York: E. P. Dutton, 1925.

Harvey, Rowland Hill. *Samuel Gompers: Champion of the Toiling Masses*. New York: Octagon Books, 1975.

Kaufman, Stuart Bruce. *Samuel Gompers and the Origins of the American Federation of Labor, 1848–1896*. Westport, CT: Greenwood Press, 1973.

Livesay, Harold C. *Samuel Gompers and Organized Labor in America*. Prospect Heights, IL: Waveland Press, 1993.

Mandel, Bernard. *Samuel Gompers*. Yellow Springs, OH: Antioch Press, 1963.

Stearn, Gerald Emanuel, ed. *Gompers*. Englewood Cliffs, NJ: Prentice-Hall, 1971.

Taft, Philip. *The A.F. of L. in the Time of Gompers*. New York: Harper & Brothers, 1957.

Thorne, Florence Calvert. *Samuel Gompers: American Statesman*. New York: Greenwood Press, 1957.

Weisberger, Bernard A. *Samuel Gompers*. Morristown, NJ: Silver Burdett, 1967.

JOURNALS AND NEWSPAPERS

Advocate of Peace

American Federationist

Billings (Montana) *Gazette*

Chicago Tribune

Industrial Pioneer

International Teamster

Ladies' Garment Worker

Literary Digest

Logansport (Indiana) *Pharos-Tribune*

Los Angeles Herald

Mark Twain Journal

McClure's Magazine

Monthly Labor Review

The Nation

New York Times

New Yorker Volkszeitung

Pearson's Magazine

Pittsburg Press

Princeton (Minnesota) *Union*

Quarterly Journal of Economics

Rocky Mountain News

Salt Lake Telegram

San Francisco Chronicle

Social Contract

The Survey

Washington Evening Star

Washington Herald

Washington Times

WEBSITES*

teachingamericanhistory.org/past-programs/hfotw/120401-2/
A project of Ashbrook University that presents online resources from American history

antiwar.com/orig/bender.php?articleid=4335
A project of the Randolph Bourne Institute providing anti-war news

firstworldwar.com/source/usconscription_gompers.htm
A site that provides useful information for students about the First World War

genpals.co.uk
A British-based service for genealogy and family history research

gompers.umd.edu/intro10.htm
gompers.umd.edu/intro11.htm
gompers.umd.edu/IWW.htm
Comprehensive site about Samuel Gompers and The Samuel Gompers Papers Project

goodreads.com/quotes/109897
Largest internet site for book readers

let.rug.nl/usa/documents/1876-1900/william-jennings-bryan-cross-of-gold-speech-july-8-1896.php
Information on American history including essays, documents and biographies

massaflcio.org
The official site of the Massachusetts AFL-CIO

pbs.org/wnet/historyofus/web09/features/source/docs/C14.pdf
PBS site for their television series, *A History of US*

presidency.ucsb.edu/ws/?pid=65402
Site of University of California Santa Barbara's American Presidency Project

prnewswire.com/news-releases/pennsylvania-afl-cio-labor-day-is-our-holiday-128697978.html
Site provides news articles and news releases for media organizations

whitehouse.gov/1600/presidents//woodrowwilson
Official White House site with information on U.S. Presidents and the presidency

* *Websites active at time of publication*

INDEX

Page numbers in **boldface** refer to images and/or captions.

A

Afel (ship), 79
Albany (NY), 28, 29
Amalgamated Association of Iron and Steel Workers
    (AA), 40
American Anti-Boycott Association, 54
American Anti-Imperialist League, 51
American Federation of Labor (AFL)
    building, 40, 48, **69**, 70, 72
    founding, 35–36
    in Atlantic City, 78
    in Buffalo, 73
    in Indianapolis, 46, 47, 48
    in Jamestown, 94
    in New York City, 46
    leaders, **70**
    seal, **19**, 35, **54**
        in Washington, D.C., 49, **92**
American Federationist, 46, 54, 55, 64, 91, 97
    See also We Don't Patronize (column)
American Labor Mission, 74
American Railway Union (ARU), 43, 44
Anarchists, 29, 34, 35, 43, 45, 59, 80, 85
Ancient Order of Foresters, 14
Antin, Mary, **75**
Arion Base Ball and Social Club, 9
Armour & Company, **16**
Arras, 76
Atlantic City, 78
Baker, Newton D., 74
Lord Balfour, 78

B

Baruch, Bernard, 72
Berkman, Alexander, 43
Berlin (ship), 47
Blue Island (IL), **44**
Boston Police Strike, 80, 81–82
Bridgeport (CT), **73**
British Trades Union Congress, 46, 47
Brooklyn, 13, 25
    Brooklyn City Hall, 13
Brotherhood of Carpenters and Joiners of America, 38
Bryan, William Jennings, 50
Buckingham Palace, 75

Buck's Stove and Range Case, 55, 62
Bureau of Labor, 29
    See also United States Department of the Interior
Burns, William J., 65–66

C

Calles, Plutarco Elias, 89, 91
Cambrai, 76
Cannon, Joseph "Uncle Joe", 60
Cardiff (Wales), 47
Carnegie, Andrew, 41
Carnegie Steel Company
    See Homestead Works
Carranza, Venustiano, 72
Castle Garden, (NY), 8, **8**
Chamber of Commerce (Boston), 82
Child labor, 18, 20, **61**, 68, 80, **86**, 87, 95
Child Labor Amendment, 87
Chinese Exclusion Act, 51, 85
Chinese immigration, 51, 52, 85
Cigar Makers' Society (London), 8
Cigarmakers' International Union, 14, 19–20, 23, 27, 28, 31
    Benefits to workers, 23, 28
    Local 15, 10, 22
    Local 144, 23, 24, 25, 26, 27, 30, 36
Cigar makers' National Union, 10
Cigar makers' Progressive Union, 30
Cigar making, **12**, **15**, **23**
    techniques, 10–12, **12**
Cigar molds, 21, 22, 23, **23**
Clark, James Beauchamp "Champ," 67
Clayton Antitrust Act, 68, 84
Cleveland, Grover
    Governor, 29
    President, 43–45
Clinton Place (NYC), 40
Committee for Industrial Organization, 95
Congress of Industrial Organizations (CIO), 95
Connecticut, 18
Coolidge, Calvin, 81
Cooper, Peter, **9**
Cooper Union, 9, **9**, 28, 51
Cornell University, 58
Council of National Defense, 72
    Committee on Labor, 72
Cuba, 51, 78
    Gompers visit to, 51
    See Havana
    See Jose Marti
    See Maine (ship)

D

Danbury (Connecticut), 54
Danbury Hatters case, 54–55
Daniels, Josephus, 78
Darrow, Clarence, 66
Dawson Lodge #16
    See Freemasons
Debs, Eugene V.
    See American Railway Union (ARU)
Democratic National Convention, 89
Derby (England), 75
Detroit, 52
Dickens, Charles, 28
Dominican Republic, 86
Draft riots, Civil War, 8–9
Dunbar, U.S.J., **90**
Duncan, James, 38, 52, **70**, 74, 78, 91, 93

E

East End (London), 5
Eight-hour movement, 19–22, 34–35, 39, **39**, 45, 60, 67, 68, 74, 95, **96**
El Paso (Texas), 89, 92
Ellis Island, **8**
Elks Lodge (NY), 92
Engels, Friedrich, 15
Executive Committee (of AFL), 36, 37, 38

F

Federation of Organized Trades and Labor Unions
    (FOTLU), 31, 33, 34–35, 36
Fort Street (London)
    See Spitalfields
Freemasonry, 53, 85, 91
Frick, Henry Clay
    See Homestead Works
King George V, 75

G

Gompers, Abraham (son), 25
Gompers, Alexander (brother), 5, 79
Gompers, Alexander (son), 25, 49
    arrest, 47
Gompers, Florence (cousin), 76
Gompers, Florence (granddaughter), 53, 70, 89
Gompers, Gertrude (second wife), 83, **84**, 88
Gompers, Harriett (sister), 5
Gompers, Henry (brother), 5
Gompers, Henry (son), 25, 49
    engraves cornerstone of AFL Building, 69–70
    first AFL office boy, 36, 38
Gompers, Jacob (brother), 5

Gompers, Louis (brother), 5
Gompers, Louis (cousin), 76
Gompers, Rosetta (Rose) (daughter), 25, 49, 52
Gompers, Sadie (daughter), 31, 49, 53, 62, 76, 84
    death of, 79
    theater experience, 77, **77**
Gompers, Samuel, 14, **18**, **38**, **50**, 56, **56**, 57, 58, **58**, **60**, **62**, **67**, **69**, **70**, 74, 76, **76**, **84**, **86**, **88**, **89**, **90**, **92**
    attends Cooper Union, 9
    attends Jewish Free School, 7
    becomes citizen, 14
    childhood in London, 5, 6, **6**, 7
    childhood in New York, 9, 10
    cigarmaker experiences, 10–16
    death, 91, 92, **92**, 93
    European travels, 47, 74, 75, 76, 77
    fraternal organizations, 14, 53
    health, 79, 82, 88, 89
    influence of Karl Laurrell, 15
    marriage to Gertrude Neuscheler, 83
    marriage to Sophia Julian, 13
    postage stamp, 96
    President of AFL, 36, 37–38, 46, 47–48, 50, **50**, 53
    President of FOTLU, 33, 35
Gompers, Samuel (son), 25, 39, 70, 79, 89
Gompers, Sarah (mother), 5
Gompers, Solomon (father), 5, 6, 7, 70, 82
    arrival in New York City, 8–9
Gompers, Sophia (first wife), 13, 47, 52, 62, **62**, **75**, 79, 84
    family hardships, 14, 25, 31, 36, 39, 40
    death, 82, 83
Government Printing Office, 49
de Graffenried, Clare, 28–29
Granite Cutters National Union, 38, 52, 70
Grant, Ulysses S., 14, 22–23, **96**
Green, William, 90

H

Hackensack (NJ), 13
Haig, Sir Douglas, 76
Hand-in-Hand Society, 14, 25, 36, 40, **54**
Harding, Warren, 81
Harvard University, 58
Hatters' Days, 55
Havana, 51
Hay, John, 51
Haymarket riot, 34, **34**, 35, **35**
Haywood, William "Big Bill," 59, **60**
Hirsch, David, 14

Homestead Steel Strike, 41, **41, 42**
Homestead Works, 40, 43
Homestead, PA, 40, **41, 42**
Huguenots, 6
Hurst, George, 24
Hutchinson, Matthew, 25

I
Immigration Act of 1924, 85
Indianapolis, 46, 47, 48, 65
Independent Order of Odd Fellows, 14
Industrial Workers of the World (IWW), **33**, 59, **59, 60**
Injunctions, 44, 54, 61, 67, 84
International Association of Bridge and Structural
    Iron Workers, 66
International Federation of Trade Unions, 79
International Labor Commission
    See International Labour Organization (ILO)
International Labor Organization (ILO), 78
International Ladies' Garment Workers' Union, 90
International Typographical Union, 38
    Women's Auxiliary, **61**
Iowa, 52

J
Jamestown (VA), 94
Jews' Free School, 7, **7**
Jones' Wood (NY), 40
Journeymen Tailors' Union of America, 38
Juárez (Mexico), 90
Julian, Sophia
    See Gompers, Sophia

K
Knights of Labor, 19, 20, 30, 31, 32, 33, **33**, 35

L
Labor Day, 45, **45, 61**, 74
Labor's Bill of Grievances, 59, 68
Landsmanschaftn, 14
Laurrell, Karl, 15, 16, 27
Lawrence (MA), 58
Le Bosse, Clara Gompers (Aunt), 75
Lennon, John B., 38, **70**
Lewis, John L, 87
Lincoln, Abraham, 10
London (ship), 8
London (city), 5, **6**, 9, 10, 13, 47, 74, 75, 76
    See also Spitalfields
Los Angeles Times Bombing, 65–66, **65**
Loewe & Company, 54
Lower East Side (NYC), 5, 9, 22
Lusitania (ship), 72

M
McBride, John, 46, 47
McCormick Harvesting Machine Company, 34
McGuire, Peter J., 38, 47
McKees Rock (PA), **64**
McKinley, William, 50, 52
McNamara, James B., 66, 67
McNamara, John J., 66, 67
Maine (ship)
    See Spanish American War
Martí, José, 51
Marx, Karl, 15
Queen Mary, 75
Mexican Federation of Labor, 90, 91
Mexico, 72, 78, 86, 89, 90, 91
Missanabie (ship), 74
Mitchell, John, 52, 55, 62, **70**
Mitchell, Rose Gompers
    See Gompers, Rose
Morris, Max, **70**
Morrison, Frank, 38, 55, 62, **70**, 91
Morrison, John, 52

N
National Child Labor Committee, 87
National Civic Federation (NCF), 52, 53, 58
National Labor Union (NLU), 19, 31
Neuscheler, Gertude
    See Gompers, Gertrude
New York City, 5, 8, **8**, 9, 10, **10, 11**, 14, **20**, 21, 23, **23**,
    24, 28, 29, 36, 39, 45, **45**, 46, 47, 49, 51, 52, **54**, 58, **61**,
    63, **63, 68**, 69, **75**, 77, 79, 88, 91, 92, 93
New York State Legislature, 29, 53
Night Free School (London), 7

O
Ouray Building, 49

P
Padua (Italy), 76
Pan-American Federation of Labor, 78, 86, 89, 91
Panama Canal, 86
Paris Peace Conference, 78
Park Theatre (Brooklyn), 13
Pennsylvania National Guard, 42, **42**
Philadelphia, 18–19, 79
Philippines
    See Spanish-American War
Pinkertons, 41, **41**, 42
Pinkerton National Detective Agency
    See Pinkertons
Pittsburgh, 31, 40

Plank 10, 46

Poudrette; or, Under the Snow, 13

Powderly, Terence, 32, 33, **33**

Prohibition, 87, **87**, 88, **88**

Pullman, George, 43

Pullman's Palace Car Company, 43

Pullman strike, 43–44, **44**, 54

"pure and simple" unionism, 95

Q

Queen Elizabeth (ship), **76**

R

Railroad Strikes

    in 1877, **30**

    in 1894, 43–44, **44**

Raleigh Hotel, **84**

Red Scare, 80

Remington Arms Factory, **73**

Rock Island Railroad, **44**

Roosevelt, Theodore

    Assemblyman, 29

    President, 53, 55, 59, 60

Rosenwald, Julius, 72

Rotterdam (ship), 79

Russian Revolution, 79

S

Schuylkill River (PA), **87**

Sears, Roebuck & Company, 72

Sherman Antitrust Act, 54, 55, 68

Shirtwaist Workers' Strike

    See Uprising of the 20,000

Sigman, Morris, 90

Sleepy Hollow Cemetery (NY), 93

Socialism and socialists, 14, 15, 29, 30, 45, 46, 59, 75, 78, 79, 80, 85, 86, 95

Spanish-American War, 51, 52

Spanish Flu, 77

Spitalfields, 5, 6, **6**, 74

St. Louis (MO), 55

Stachelberg, Michael, 11

    cigar shop, 13

Stove Mounters' International Union Label, **64**

Strasser, Adolph, 22, 23, 28, 30, 31

Strikes, 10, 14, 16, 18, 20, 21, 23, 31, 32, 34, 40, **60**, **64**, 68, **68**, 69, 80, 81, **81**, 84, **84**, **86**

    Boston Police, 81

    cigar industry, 24–26, 27, 29

    garment industry, 63, **63**

    Homestead, **41**, 41–43

    Loewe & Company, 54–55

    Pullman, 43–44, **44**, 54

Railroad, **30**, 44

    Steelworkers, 80, **81**

Suffrage, 84, **85**

T

Taft, William Howard, 67–68

Tenadores (ship), 77

Tenement manufacturing, **10**, 22, 24, 28, 29, 53

    Tenement Cigar Strike (1877), 24, 25

Thompsonville Carpet Manufacturing Company, 18

Thorne, Florence, 91

"To the West, To the West, To the Land of the Free" (Song), 8

Tompkins Square riot, **20**, 21

Trade Union Advocate, 38, 46

Typographical Temple, 49

U

Under the Snow

    See Poudrette

United Cigar Makers of New York (UCMNY), 22, 23

United Garment Workers of America, 46

Union label, **19**, 64, **64**

United Mine Workers (UMW), 46, 52, 55, 87, 95

United Nations, 78

United States Department of Labor, 68

United States Department of the Interior, 29

    See also Bureau of Labor

United States House of Representatives, 39, 67

    Committee on Labor, 39

United States Senate, 67, 80, 92

United States Steel, 80

United States Supreme Court, 44, 54, 55, 63, 68

Union Station, **92**

Uprising of the 20,000, 63

V

Van Buren, Martin, 18

King Victor Emmanuel, 76

W

Washington Cemetery (NY), 77

Washington, DC, 22, 39, 48, 49, **50**, 52–53, 62, 69, **69**, 70, **84**, **88**, 89, 91, 92, **92**

We Don't Patronize (column), 54, 55

Welzmiller, Mrs. Louis Reed, **75**

Wilson, William B., 68

Wilson, Woodrow, 57, 67, 68, **69**, 70, 71, 72, 73, 74, 77, 78, 79, 80, **85**

Wise, Rabbi Stephen S., 92

Wobblies

    See Industrial Workers of the World (IWW)

World War I, 71, 72, **73**, 74, 75, **75**, 76, **76**, 77, 80, **81**

PICTURE CREDITS